JHU

FACING PHYSICAL VIOLENCE

Glynis Breakwell

Problems in Practice

This series is the natural successor to the popular *Psychology in Action* series, and continues and extends the aim of 'giving psychology away', that is, making psychological expertise more freely available.

Each title focuses on a common problem across a number of different professions – industry, education, medicine, the police and other public and social services. The approach is practical, drawing on examples from a range of work situations. And the reader is constantly invited to look at the problem both as object and subject: accepting help as well as offering help; dealing with your own aggressive impulses as well as those directed towards you by others; both giving and requesting expert advice. Psychologists have a great deal to say about how to improve our working lives and the aim here is to offer both practical skills and new insights.

THE AUTHORS AND EDITORS

Glynis Breakwell (Senior Lecturer in Psychology, University of Surrey, Guildford)

David Fontana (Reader in Educational Psychology, University of Wales College of Cardiff)

Glenys Parry (Regional Tutor in Clinical Psychology, Knowle Hospital, Fareham and Top Grade Clinical Psychologist, Department of Psychotherapy, Royal South Hants Hospital, Southampton)

The original, problem-solving approach of this series was applied also to the creation of these titles, by a team of three, acting as both authors and editors. Each member of the team, drawing on their own practical experience, contributed ideas, material and criticism to every title, in addition to taking full responsibility for the writing of at least one of them. This approach ensures a book of wide practical relevance, combining the strengths and expertise of all authors, a uniformity of approach with a minimum of overlap between titles, yet retaining the clear, simple line of the single-authored book. The commitment of the authors to the series made all of this possible.

OTHER TITLES IN THE SERIES

Facing Physical Violence by Glynis Breakwell
Working Through Crises by Glenys Parry
Interviewing by Glynis Breakwell

Problems in Practice

FACING PHYSICAL VIOLENCE

Glynis M. Breakwell

Department of Psychology
University of Surrey

BPS
BOOKS

Published by The British Psychological Society
and Routledge Ltd.

First published in 1989 by The British Psychological Society, St Andrews House, 48 Princess Road East,Leicester, LE1 7DR, in association with Routledge Ltd, 11 New Fetter Lane, London EC4P 4EE, and in the USA with Chapman & Hall Inc., 29 West 35th Street, New York NY 10001.

British Library Cataloguing in Publication Data

Breakwell, Glynis M.
    Facing physical violence. – (Problems in practice).
    1. Professional personnel.
    Violence by clients
    I. Title II. Series
    331.7'12'0941

    ISBN 0–901715–96–4
    ISBN 0–901715–95–6 pbk

Printed and bound in Great Britain by Biddles Ltd, Guildford.
Whilst every effort has been made to ensure the accuracy of the contents of this publication, the publishers and authors expressly disclaim responsibility in law for negligence or any other cause of action whatsoever.

To Colin Rowett,
whose study of violence against social workers
made a real contribution to our knowledge

Contents

INTRODUCTION TO THE SERIES   ii

FOREWORD   x

1. WHAT DO PRACTITIONERS WANT TO KNOW?   1

Analysing the problem   5
The possibility of change   6
Self-assessment exercises   6

2. VIOLENCE AND AGGRESSION IN THE CONTEXT OF CARING   7

Assertiveness, aggression and violence   8
Violence: an occupational hazard   9
The paradox of caring and control   14
    Dangers of the controlling relationship   15
    Dangers of the caring relationship   17
    Working with powerful emotions   17
Practitioner violence   19
Stress and violence   20
Stress and the caring professions   25
    Coping with stress   25

3. COMMON FEATURES OF ATTACKS AND EXPLANATIONS OF VIOLENCE   28

Violence in the health services   28
Violence in the social services   32
Violence in schools   40
    Incidence and features of attacks: some conclusions   43
Explanations of aggression and violence   43
    Interpreting situations   50
    Violence in a group context   51
Anticipating what kind of violence   52
    General and specific clues   53

4. AVOIDANCE, ESCAPE AND CONTROL   56

Underlying objectives   56

Strategies of avoidance   57
    Predicting violence   57
    Calculating risks   61
Protection and escape   65
    Organisational strategies   65
    Self-help strategies   66
    Anxiety management   68
Controlling a violent situation   69
In conclusion . . .   71

5. LIFE AFTER ATTACK   72

Typical reactions after assault   72
    Fear, surprise, anger and guilt   74
Victimisation   76
    Facing victimisation   78
    The role of the popular press   79

6. POLICY AND MANAGEMENT   81

Guidelines for practice   81
Support for staff   82
Structured training   83
Providing safeguards   84
    The value of collaboration   86

CONCLUSION   87

References   91
Further Reading   93
Index   95

Self-Assessment Exercises:

1. Aggression and Violence Outside Work   9

2. Tolerable Aggression and Violence   12

3. The Stress Checklist   22

4. Features of Attacks   34

5. Personally Preferred Forms of Aggression or Violence   46

6. The Dangerousness Checklist   59

Foreword

The *Psychology in Practice* series of books offers those working in managerial, caring and other professions practical psychological guidance on a number of topics of central concern to their work. Based upon solid research evidence (demonstrating that the usefulness of applied psychology depends on proven data), the series nevertheless avoids burdening the reader with lists of references and research dates, and concentrates firmly upon the application of psychological knowledge to real-life situations.

In *Facing Physical Violence* Glynis Breakwell tackles the problem of how best to manage violence. As she tells us in her opening chapter, the threat of such violence is causing increasing concern, particularly in the caring professions, as practitioners become aware that they may be at risk of being physically abused by the very people whom they are trying to help. Faced with such threats, practitioners need to answer such questions as: when are these attacks most likely to occur? what skills are necessary to avoid or cope with them? and what can be done in the aftermath of an attack to help us cope with the traumas involved?

Calling upon her considerable experience of working with people exposed to violence, Glynis Breakwell sets out to provide the answers to these and similar questions. But she warns us that such answers are not simple, since violence is a complex multicausal issue, in which the practitioner can be implicated. Accordingly she offers us two kinds of help. Firstly she outlines what it is in us, as professionals, which may invite others to be violent, and discusses how best we can change our behaviour so that we can work with the powerful emotions experienced by those we are trying to help without inviting unnecessary risk. And secondly she discusses both how we may predict which situations are likely to be dangerous and how we may defuse actual encounters which are turning nasty.

The emphasis throughout the book, as indeed throughout the series, is upon *practical* issues. The author presupposes no specialist psychological knowledge on the part of her readers, and talks directly to both experienced and novice practitioners. Her tone is supportive and reassuring, and her message is that physical violence, no matter how intimidating in prospect (she offers us some disturbing accounts of death and serious injuries in practitioners at the hands of aggressive clients), can be coped with and in the great majority of cases avoided through the observation of sensible guidelines.

Because this is a practical book, Glynis Breakwell includes a number of self-assessment exercises designed to help you to gauge such things as the degree of violence which you deem acceptable (perhaps surprisingly there is a wide variation amongst practitioners), your own characteristic way of expressing violence (yes we can experience violent emotions too!) and the actual extent of the violence we have encountered in our professional lives. There is also a valuable self-assessment exercise aimed at helping us identify our professional stress levels, since the more stressed we are the less able we are to cope with the violence in other people and the more likely we are to give way to emotional outbursts ourselves.

It is sometimes fashionable these days to outline at the start of a book the precise ways in which the reader's behaviour will be changed by reading it. I would say of this book that by the end of it you will not only have a much better idea of when and where and why physical violence occurs at work, but also a much clearer idea of how to anticipate, avoid or cope with violence itself. Out of this learning will come a much greater professional confidence. We all of us as practitioners fear violence, not only for the physical and psychological damage it can do but also for the aggressive emotions it may in turn arouse in ourselves. With the help of this book we can lay a large part of that fear to rest, and in consequence face our working lives with greater equanimity and – dare I say it? – enjoyment and enthusiasm.

David Fontana and Glenys Parry
Series editors

Chapter One

What Do Practitioners Want to Know?

The purpose of this book is to discuss a problem which is greatly occupying the caring professions: violent attacks against practitioners by their clients. Increasingly, members of the caring professions, such as social workers, counsellors, psychologists, health visitors, nurses, doctors and teachers, are aware that they are at risk from their clients, patients or pupils during the normal course of their work. The seriousness of the problem has been highlighted by the killings of four social workers and one health visitor.

▶ James Gray, a social work specialist for the deaf in Southampton, was stabbed to death by a male client who was deaf and dumb in July 1978.

▶ Carolyn Puckett, a health visitor for Oxford City Council, was killed in March 1980 by the father of the family she had been visiting. Her charred body was found in the burnt-out remains of her car.

▶ Isabel Schwarz, a social worker, was killed in Bexley Hospital where she worked in July 1984 by an ex-client. The killer, a woman who was known to be seriously mentally ill, stabbed Isabel Schwarz 39 times.

▶ In 1985, Norma Morris, a Haringey social worker, was hacked to death in broad daylight by a youth she was visiting who had previously tried to commit suicide.

▶ In September 1986, Frances Bettridge, a Birmingham social worker, and the client that she was visiting were strangled by the client's common-law husband, who then attempted to burn their bodies.

These cases have received much media and professional attention. There are undoubtedly others which have not attracted the same sort of examination. Social workers and health visitors are currently to the fore in discussions about violence but other professions have also suffered fatalities. For instance, between 1976 and 1978, one GP (general practitioner) and two consultant psychiatrists were killed; in these cases the murderers were paranoid schizophrenics who held specific delusions about their doctors.

Death appears to be merely the most painful tip of an iceberg – though a more appropriate metaphor might be that of a volcano. Reports of attacks and injuries which are serious but not ultimately life threatening are readily available. For instance, in October 1986, Jean Rainey, a social worker for Southwark, was attacked with a meat cleaver by a client who had a history of psychiatric disturbance. She sustained serious injuries to her head and leg. Earlier in 1986, a 47-year-old social worker was raped, stabbed and robbed in her own office by a 17-year-old client.

Such attacks are not restricted to female practitioners. A male GP, Dr Cembrowicz, described in the *British Medical Journal* in 1987 how he had been punched and kicked by a patient, resulting in a scrotal haematoma which necessitated two weeks off work. Nor are they restricted to the health and social services. In a survey of school teachers conducted by the National Association of Schoolmasters and Union of Women Teachers (1986) one male teacher reported being attacked seven times over a period of fourteen years: once with a knife, once with a stiletto, once with an air rifle, once when a pupil fed gas into his classroom while he was teaching, twice when pupils used their fists, and once when an ex-pupil tried to run him over with a car.

The problem of violence is of growing concern, particularly in the caring professions, as practitioners become aware that they may be at risk of being physically abused by the very people whom they believe they are trying to help. This abuse is not always acute and easily visible; it is sometimes chronic but minor, extending over long periods of time. For instance, many nurses will attest to the difficulties of bathtime on geriatric wards or in homes for the elderly. Their often confused or dementing patients will bruise and scratch them in an effort to escape the unwanted but needed assistance in keeping themselves clean. Other members of the caring professions would attest to the frequently severe challenging behaviour of some mentally handicapped people.

In the context of the increased visibility of such assaults and the real anxiety they can provoke, practitioners and their employers alike want to know:

1. HOW FREQUENT ARE VIOLENT ATTACKS AND PHYSICAL ABUSE?

There have been quite contradictory reports about the frequency and pattern of client violence. Accounts vary within each profession. Estimates for social work vary widely from 1 in every 4 social workers being attacked to only 1 in 25,000. There also seems to be great diversity between different sorts of practitioner in the form and frequency of violence encountered. For instance, despite much rumour to the contrary, teachers, according to recent research, seem rarely to experience physical violence but do have to face regular verbal abuse as part of frequent but trivial misbehaviour in the classroom.

2. HOW DO SUCH ATTACKS OCCUR?

The professions want to know where and when such violence is likely. They also want to know which sorts of people are most likely to be involved: who are the victims and who are the attackers?

3. HOW CAN ATTACKS BE EXPLAINED?

People want to understand why they happen. They want to know what goes wrong, and in particular who can be blamed. They want to tap into the social and psychological processes which generate such violence.

There seems to be some assumption that explanation will lead to prevention. This may be a false assumption. Explanation may help prediction but knowing the cause of an act of violence is only useful if, as a result, it is possible to remove the cause. Some causes can be eradicated. For instance, the repetition of an incident where an elderly woman becomes abusive because a male warden in a home for the elderly walks into her room without knocking may be prevented by ensuring that the privacy and territoriality of residents is respected subsequently. However, many causes of violence are not so easy to alter: violence can result from mental illness or from long-term economic deprivation; such causes cannot be removed, though they may be ameliorated.

There is a further problem with the assumption that explanation can lead to control. Where specific acts of violence *can* be explained, it often turns out that several causes have interacted with each other. In practice, it is rarely possible to anticipate how these causes interact so that they can be changed successfully.

This does not mean that explanation is pointless. It is valuable because it will enable the *prediction* of violence. Knowing what causal factors are involved in generating violence makes it possible to predict under what circumstances it is likely to occur. Prediction, in turn, makes evasion, avoidance or containment possible.

4. WHAT PROFESSIONAL SKILLS ARE NEEDED?

Practitioners want to know, first, how to avoid situations where attacks are likely and, second, how to deal with incidents when they do occur, which includes coping with their emotional and organisational aftermath.

5. WHAT ORGANISATIONAL CHANGES WOULD HELP?

Since provision for the reasonable safety of employees is a legal obligation of employers (under the 1974 Health and Safety at Work Act), most organisations are concerned to know how they should change in order to handle the possibility of physical assault upon their employees. Changes that have been considered include modifications in training, management procedures for dealing with practitioners who are at risk of being attacked or those who have been attacked, and in the provision of material resources to help practitioners, such as modifications in the physical environment in their place of work or in communication systems. A big question mark still hangs over many of these management responses. Their efficacy and economic viability have not yet been established.

NO EASY ANSWERS

In an area of such public concern, where solutions are urgently required, it is important not to be deluded into thinking that any simple panaceas are at hand. Not all the questions can currently be answered. However, the objective of this book is to provide *some* answers. It can do this by drawing upon a growing, if unsystematic, body of research on these issues, taken often from the social services but also from the educational and health services. It will also use examples of 'good' practice from social service, health and education authorities where new codes of practice and different patterns of resource provision have been introduced.

ANALYSING THE PROBLEM

The book will describe the sorts of incident that happen and the ways in which they are treated. Typically this will involve a description of: what led up to the incident, the extent of the violence and its form, how the victim of the attack felt afterwards, the reporting of incidents, management responses to them, the longer-term effects of attacks and the stereotyping of the victim by other professionals and their management. This will be accompanied by a social psychological analysis of the explanations for violence and its repercussions for practitioners who are attacked and their employing organisations. Case studies are used to illustrate the general points made.

TACTICS OF AVOIDANCE AND ESCAPE

Tactics which the practitioner can use when faced with a potentially violent client will be described. But they will not focus on techniques of physical self-defence. This is not a self-defence manual. The tactics will focus on the skills needed to read cues given by a client that an attack is likely, and on the methods that you can employ to extricate yourself. Examples of ways of getting out of difficult situations which have been used by people in the past will be discussed. The examples serve to emphasise the fact that simple, generalisable rules about how to behave in a violent situation cannot be formulated. In the light of the available information, *you* have to decide what strategies will work for you.

AFTERMATH OF ATTACK

The book will also examine the likely problems that you may experience after being involved in an attack. Some space will be devoted to the methods which can be used to restore self-confidence, cope with self-doubt and control guilt. This will include a consideration of the ways in which practitioners can be placed in a double bind situation by the demands of their jobs, which require them to follow a caring philosophy yet also require them to control and constrain their clients. The uneasy truce between these two conflicting sets of demands is shattered when the client becomes violent with the carer. The whole fabric of the caring relationship is transformed. The questions are then: how does the practitioner carry on, how is the conception of the client changed, and how are relationships with colleagues altered?

PRACTITIONER VIOLENCE TOWARDS CLIENTS

In discussing violence towards the practitioner, it would be inappropriate to ignore the violence which sometimes flows in the opposite direction: from carer to client. This also has to be discussed in order to understand the dynamics of the 'caring' relationship. Powerful emotions are at work on both sides of the caring divide and they need to be recognised.

THE POSSIBILITY OF CHANGE

This is not a 'cookbook' on how to cope with violence exhibited by clients. Some suggestions will inevitably be examined but that is not the main aim. Instead, the book is designed to enable you to understand what is happening, to recognise that it happens to lots of people, that the pattern of events is similar, that the emotions experienced are commonly shared, and that the whole process is not inevitable – practitioners *can* bring about change.

SELF-ASSESSMENT EXERCISES AND SCENARIOS

At various points throughout the book self-assessment exercises are included. Their purpose is to demonstrate the personal relevance of the general arguments being made. They are designed to encourage you to reflect upon your own experiences of violence or aggression and your feelings about them. If completed sequentially, they build up to give a general picture of involvement in, reactions to and understanding of aggressive or violent incidents. They can be used to monitor change too; the self-assessment can be repeated after an interval of perhaps a year or after a particularly significant incident in practice. As long as the originals are retained for comparison, it is possible to identify areas of change. If changes are occurring, whether positive or negative, the objective is to pinpoint the likely reasons so as to improve your chances of controlling the nature of future changes.

A series of hypothetical scenarios is also presented. These are designed to illustrate some of the principles outlined in the text. Normally, they will ask you to say what you would do in the situation outlined and then offer guidelines about the alternative courses of action available. Again, it is possible to use these scenarios to monitor changes in your perspective over time.

Both the self-assessment exercises and the scenarios are designed primarily to be used by individual readers. They can, however, be used by groups, for instance in training workshops.

Chapter Two

Violence and Aggression in the Context of Caring

Violence is a regular fact of life for many people; experience of aggression is an everyday event for most, if only at second hand. In focusing upon problems experienced by the caring professions it is possible to miss how pervasive aggression and violence are in *all* human exchanges.

Of course, this is most evident in cataclysmic conflicts between different groups of people: over the last 5,600 years of recorded history, humanity has averaged three wars per year (Montagu, 1976). It is also reflected in the crime statistics: in the United States during this century over 10,000 people per year have died as a result of criminal acts, a rate approximately nine times greater than that in western European nations.

Perhaps most importantly, violence is manifest in family life. A national survey in America done in 1980 (Straus *et al.*) showed that 1 in 6 households in the previous year had seen one partner hit the other and in 3 in 5, where children were resident, parents had hit their children. In Britain, Scott (1977) after reviewing the available evidence, concluded that between 1 and 12 children in every 1,000 are abused by their parents. (The variation in the estimates resulted from disparities in the definition of abuse adopted in the study and the differences in the ages of the children considered.) The extent of wife battering in England and Wales is suggested by the number of court injunctions granted to wives against husbands who have assaulted them. In a single 18-month period, nearly 9,000 injunctions were recorded. This is clearly likely to be an underestimate of actual violence within marriage, since many assaults go unreported.

It is in the context of a violent society that violence to the caring professions must be examined. The caring professions probably need reminding of this less than other groups because they are the people mainly involved in dealing with the consequences of other people's violence. They pick up the pieces of lives shattered by violence behind closed doors in leafy suburbia, or injured by crime on the streets, hooliganism on the terraces or terrorism in the air.

ASSERTIVENESS, AGGRESSION AND VIOLENCE

It is important to start with a precise definition of the terms 'assertiveness', 'aggression' and 'violence'. In everyday conversation the demarcation lines between them are often blurred and this can become confusing when analysing how to deal with these three types of behaviour. What they share is that they all involve confrontation. They differ in the form of, and motivation for, the confrontation.

ASSERTIVENESS entails insisting on your rights or opinions; it involves claiming recognition from others that, within the constraints of the law, you have the right to decide how you will think, feel and act.

AGGRESSION is typically defined by psychologists as any form of behaviour intended to harm or injure someone else against his or her wishes. This means that intentionally harming someone else is not aggression if the injured party wanted it to happen. Aggression entails any form of injury – psychological or emotional included. So belittling, cursing, shaming, frightening or threatening can all constitute aggression.

VIOLENCE comprises those acts in which there is a deliberate attempt to inflict physical harm. Thus *accidental* harm does not comprise violence. For example, damage which is a by-product of anger but is not intended does not comprise violence. It may feel the same to the victim but it cannot be explained in the same way as deliberate attempts to harm. This distinction between intended and accidental outcomes is made in our everyday lives and in the legal system. We make it in deciding how we react to the individual causing the damage. We need to bear it in mind in explaining and predicting violence.

The distinction between assertiveness and aggression is worth emphasising in the context of the activities of the caring professions. Being able to be assertive is important for many of the people with whom these professionals deal. It is the means whereby individuality and identity are constructed and maintained, often in situations where

AGGRESSION AND VIOLENCE OUTSIDE WORK

While accepting that violence and aggression are all too prevalent among other people, many individuals will deny that they have a part in their own lives. The purpose of this exercise is for you to examine your life to check whether they are part of **your** experience. For the moment, focus only upon incidents that have taken place outside work in which you have been the victim.

Break your life into four periods: your childhood, adolescence, adulthood until recently, and now.

For each period list:

1. what types of violence or aggression you have experienced;

2. which people acted as aggressors in each case;

3. the context in which the events occurred;

4. how frequently each type of incident occurred.

There are no figures for a representative sample of the population against which you can compare your own experience of violence or aggression. The value of doing the exercise lies not in establishing how typical your experience is. Instead, it establishes the backdrop for appreciating how experiences of aggression or violence at work may relate to earlier or current experiences outside your working life. It brings to the surface recollections of unpleasant events which may colour how you deal with aggression or violence in practice. It is useful to consider how these experiences outside the caring context influence what you think, feel and do inside it.

If you have a history of having to deal with aggression, do you have some incipient belief that you have become the perpetual victim? Or have you worked up strategies for deflection and survival? If you have no experience of violence outside your working life, do you feel immune at work or do you feel anxious that you would not know what to do? The answers to these questions differ across people. The important thing is to know the answer which you would give, whatever that answer happens to be.

both are attacked. The process of institutionalisation has been described in many of the contexts in which carers work, especially in hospitals and hostels. It involves the gradual disintegration of individuality as the person conforms more and more to the requirements of the institution's regime. It has advantages for the institution in that it makes management of the patient or resident easier but there are costs too. Independence and self-reliance decay and the chances of recovery or rehabilitation are eroded. Assertiveness can be used as an antidote to the effects of institutionalisation.

Assertiveness is not only important within institutions, it is useful for clients in the community. Much social work and counselling would be unnecessary if clients were capable of being assertive in the pursuit of their own rights in such areas as employment, housing or welfare benefits. Most teachers would see the propagation of assertiveness as a major task for education.

However, while assertiveness in the spirit may be valued, there is often a problem in the flesh. This is because assertiveness can slip into aggression. Often people do not know how to claim their own rights except through attacking those of others. Sometimes when assertiveness fails to achieve the desired recognition of their rights people may become aggressive. Being successfully assertive without being aggressive takes great skill. It is a skill which all carers need to acquire. Carers need to be assertive on their own behalf with their clients, patients, or pupils. They also need to be assertive with other people and with institutions on behalf of those for whom they care.

VIOLENCE: AN OCCUPATIONAL HAZARD

In 1975, a senior social worker in Bedfordshire was attacked by a client and his wife and nearly strangled to death. She was visiting them in connection with a suspected non-accidental injury suffered by their baby; two of their four children had already been taken from the couple. About 12 months before, another social worker had been released unharmed after being imprisoned for 21 hours in a caravan with a home-made guillotine over his neck; his captor was armed with three guns. At roughly the same time, in Belfast an assistant principal social worker had his face lacerated and his eyes blackened after a schizophrenic woman client he was visiting threw a peat briquette at him.

All these examples come from social work, but they could equally well have been drawn from other caring professions. In August 1975, the Confederation of Health Services Employees had on file more than 90 claims for compensation resulting from attacks on nurses and orderlies.

At the time, violence was being described as an occupational hazard: if you are dealing with disturbed or difficult people, managers in the caring professions claimed, you can expect to face physical violence. Even the practitioners being attacked echoed this acceptance of the inevitability of what might be called *vocational violence*.

TOLERABLE AGGRESSION

A norm is a standard which reflects what is considered the customary or expected behaviour for a particular situation or group of people. There seem to be reasonably strong norms about the nature of violence and aggression within the caring professions. These centre upon what might be called *tolerable aggression*. Most of the caring professions hold values which accept that a certain amount of aggression is to be expected from those in their care. Nurses freely acknowledge that patients in pain or in fear will become abusive, truculent and often physically dangerous. Teachers talk about the disruption and border-line threats of physical assault (the shoving, jostling horseplay which hovers around really serious attempts to injure) which they know they must anticipate from certain classes. Residential social workers, especially in places, like the intermediate treatment centres, with young male residents, describe how conflicts between residents pre-dictably envelop the staff who try to intervene to resolve them. Doctors working on the accident or emergency wards of large hospitals know that the people who they treat often become aggressive. The point is that dealing with such aggression or violence has been regarded as an integral part of the carer's job. Management tends to reaffirm this: it is implied that if you want to be a doctor, nurse, social worker, teacher, or whatever, you have to expect to be faced with aggression and, in some cases, violence.

Norms of tolerable aggression undoubtedly exist in the caring pro-fessions. There is, however, doubt about whether they are stable or in a state of flux. Certainly, the recent concern about the risk of serious physical injury seems to be shifting the baseline. It seems that in most of the caring professions a critical examination of the norms is under way. Through their trade unions and professional associations, carers are calling for the risks associated with their work to be assessed. In a number of contexts this has resulted in industrial action, with calls to employers to introduce new codes of practice or new staffing arrange-

TOLERABLE AGGRESSION AND VIOLENCE

Below is a list of various types of aggression or violence, exhibited by different types of people in different sorts of situation. Since the list covers sorts of incident which occur across a number of caring professions, some may be irrelevant to your work – just ignore these.

In the first column tick those which you would currently tolerate as an acceptable part of your job and which you would not report to your manager or senior colleague. In the second column tick all those which you would have accepted when you first started to practise. In the third column, tick all those which you think that other members of your profession in general would typically tolerate.

This is not an easy task because in each case it is of course possible to argue that you cannot say what you would do in the abstract; the precise circumstances would determine your response. However, respond to the checklist in a way which reflects how you would be most likely to react or have found that you typically react.

	What you now would tolerate	What you used to tolerate	What others would tolerate
A. Where the aggressor is a child:			
Swearing/cursing			
Threats of violence			
Pushing/shoving			
Scratching			
Punching			
Kicking			
Attack with weapon			
B. Where the aggressor is an adult:			
Swearing/cursing			
Threats of violence			
Pushing/shoving			
Scratching			
Punching			
Kicking			
Attack with weapon			

	What you now would tolerate	What you used to tolerate	What others would tolerate
C. Where the aggressor is elderly:			
Swearing/cursing			
Threats of violence			
Pushing/shoving			
Scratching			
Punching			
Kicking			
Attack with weapon			
D. Where the aggressor has diminished responsibility (e.g. emotionally distraught, in extreme pain):			
Swearing/cursing			
Threats of violence			
Pushing/shoving			
Scratching			
Punching			
Kicking			
Attack with weapon			
E. Where a group of aggressors is involved:			
Swearing/cursing			
Threats of violence			
Pushing/shoving			
Scratching			
Punching			
Kicking			
Attack with weapon			

Compare any differences in your tolerance according to types of aggressor. Have your personal norms of tolerance changed, and over what period? How far do you consider yourself similar in the norms you apply to those applied by other members of your profession? It may be especially valuable to see whether your perception of the norms that others operate is accurate. You could get some idea by asking colleagues to complete the self-assessment exercise independently.

ments. A sense of vocation no longer prevents practitioners, especially in the social and welfare services, from becoming vocal in the interests of self defence. Residential workers have gone on strike, so have housing advisory officers. Aggression which was once tolerated because it was predictable, expected and, in many ways, explicable, is now a matter for public debate. The frontier between the tolerable and the intolerable is being renegotiated.

The change in what is deemed tolerable behaviour from clients, patients or pupils means that professionals are increasingly likely to report incidents which occur. This has the effect of making violence and aggression *appear* more frequent than they used to be. Whether they are or not in reality is another matter. Changes in reporting patterns will certainly raise the apparent incidence rate. These apparent increases then sensitise more people to the possibility of assault and to the fact that others are not simply tolerating it. They then inspect their own experiences for examples of incidents and when they occur are more willing to take action. There is a chain reaction within the caring professions which further modifies the accepted norms, and the range of tolerance shrinks even further.

Nevertheless, despite the increased visibility of the injustice of vocational violence, there is a sense in which its inevitability cannot be diminished. The caring professions are in the frontline against society's distress and disorder. If the penalties of unemployment and poverty increase, then those who help the poor and the unemployed have to face their frustration and their anger. If the health care services are understaffed and poorly resourced, then people working in them will face the frustration and anger of the ill and injured who are denied adequate provision. If the education system cannot ensure equality of opportunity and appropriate courses for all, educationalists will face the frustration and anger of the disillusioned and disadvantaged. If changes in welfare legislation result in hardship, benefits officers will bear the immediate brunt of the frustration and anger of those who are deprived. While practitioners may no longer accept violence as part of the cost of their vocation, the inevitability of having to face it remains undiminished.

THE PARADOX OF CARING AND CONTROL

The philosophies of most of the caring professions entail some assumption about the purpose of caring being to enable the client, patient or pupil to become self-reliant and independent. Help is offered in order to make the recipient autonomous, whether emotionally, intellectually, physically or financially. The carer repairs cracks, retrieves deficits, facilitates growth and change. Total autonomy and subsequent stability are sometimes recognised as unrealistic goals; the process of support is then extended. But the ideal is that after the treatment is given, the therapy concluded, the training complete, the recipient is fully functioning and self-determining.

DANGERS OF THE CONTROLLING RELATIONSHIP

It is supremely ironic, therefore, that most caring professions, as a matter of course, restrict the freedom and independence of their clients. This can occur because the person is deprived of important information which would make sensible, autonomous decisions feasible. For instance, patients in hospital may not be given all the information about alternative courses of treatment for their condition and allowed to choose which they prefer. Often patients report a sense of totally losing control of what happens to them. Failure to inform the patient, and the consequent failure to take account of their wishes in matters of treatment, need not be deliberate; it can be merely a product of institutional or professional routine. But regardless of its origin, it serves to accentuate the imbalance in power between patient and the practitioner. The patient loses power, the practitioner gains it.

The imbalance of power between carer and client is, in any case, already considerable. Most caring professions have considerable legal power over their charges. The types of legal power differ across groups. Some control the flow of financial benefits. Some are legally empowered to remove children from a family. Some are entitled to compulsorily consign people to a psychiatric hospital. Some can cause a child to be refused continued access to schooling. The important point is not the type of power, but the fact that such powers are in the hands of the same people who are offering help. Members of most of the caring professions are agents of social control as well as facilitators of individual well-being. In practice, this means that the client, patient or pupil and the practitioner are faced with having to negotiate a course of action within this imbalance of power. The practitioner has to face the particularly tricky task of resolving any conflict between professional philosophies that call for respect for clients' wishes, and the bureaucratic and institutional realities which call for efficient client control. The client needs to work out a strategy which will maximise the value of the help on offer while minimising the consequent loss of personal control.

In such a situation, violence against practitioners is hardly surprising. The client, patient or pupil is facing a double dose of distress: there is the original problem which resulted in the practitioner's involvement, and then there is the threat to self-determination which the practitioner comes to symbolise. Clients who are unused to responding to such threats with sophisticated argument are likely to resort to violence. Violence in this context is a way of redressing the imbalance of power.

The effect of violence upon the balance of power is recognised by both sides. Practitioners who are the victims of violence often report feeling that they have lost power. One social worker after an attack explained:

> *I felt patronised and humiliated, as though my superior position as a social worker had gone. I didn't feel angry or even hurt. I felt – I am in the caring role and look what happened.*

Clients who use violence describe how it temporarily gives them a sense of control. One young man, resident in an intermediate treatment centre, described how he had learned to terrorise the residential workers with fits of temper and unpredictable outburts:

> *I used to throw the furniture at them. Just when they all settled down and thought everything was quiet, then I'd start something. They soon learned not to push me about.*

DISPLACED VIOLENCE

The importance of power is associated with the conflict between caring and control. Another social worker voiced a common concern. This woman had taken a man's daughter away from him under a place of safety order; the man, a psychiatric patient, stoned the social worker's house, brandished a knife at her family, and later tried to burn the house down around them. The social worker wrote that she felt that she directly embodied the old debate about caring and policing, and the incidents made her question whether her values were correct. Her policing role prevented her from performing her caring duties – at least for that man.

Violence is interpreted in this sort of situation by those who are the targets as a sort of retribution for their failure as carers. Yet at the same time, the victims also know that the violence is not personalised. They become targets because they are fulfilling the controlling role. A 41-year-old social worker was attacked by a 15-year-old youth in a police station when she was quizzing him about inconsistencies in the story he had given the police about a crime. She suffered two black eyes, a chipped tooth and a bloodied nose. Her immediate reaction was to ask: 'How could anyone hate me that much?' But, she subsequently realised that: 'He had clobbered me for what I represented, not for me as a person.'

In such cases, the violence is not instrumental, and it just happens to be displaced upon the practitioner. Talk of violence being used to redress imbalances in power may tend to overestimate the extent to which it is rational or deliberate. Most clients who become violent would not expect to gain any lasting adjustment in the balance of power. Perceived powerlessness can give rise to aggression, which is then directed at the practitioner in the absence of any better or more easily accessible target.

DANGERS OF THE CARING RELATIONSHIP

Violence can be used not in response to control, but in response to care. Especially in longer-term counselling or residential care relationships, clients or patients may use violence as a means of testing the strength or safety of the relationship. The practitioner can become the object of minor but regular physical assault. In some caring professions this period of trial is deemed necessary in certain cases for the development of a therapeutic relationship.

Problems arise where the scale and significance of the attacks are underestimated. There are particular dangers when the motive for the attacks is misattributed, when they are thought to be symbolic tests and are really the preliminaries to a full-scale assault. There was a notable example of this where a patient repeatedly threatened to shoot his psychiatrist. One day the psychiatrist's receptionist reported that the patient was in the waiting room with a gun, the psychiatrist walked out of his office to greet the patient and was immediately shot. Professionalism and the desire to maintain the 'caring relationship' sometimes militate against a more practical interpretation of the situation.

WORKING WITH POWERFUL EMOTIONS

It is strange how few members of the caring professions are ever trained directly to handle powerful emotions. The caring professions occupy the frontline against distress and disorder, and it is predictable that the caring relationship will be the focal point for the expression of strong emotions, both positive and negative. Yet practitioners have minimal instruction on how to deal with these emotions. For instance, nurses and doctors who will witness everything from great joy to total desolation in their patients are taught how to cope with their physical but not their emotional reactions.

Practitioners are left to acquire an understanding of the extremes of emotional expression through on-the-job observation. Where the emotion concerned is anger or hatred, the costs of firsthand experience can be considerable. This is especially important if considered in the light of available evidence that the form which emotions take is dependent upon their social context. An individual who is emotionally aroused can be channelled into any of a range of emotions by cues present in the situation. With others who are calm and happy, the aroused person may become very happy; in contrast, if they are belligerent, the aroused person may become violent.

It is valuable to know something of the *effects* of powerful emotions. They have a great impact upon cognition – the process of information gathering, storage and handling. For instance, emotion can block the ability of the individual to understand new instructions; it can result in memory failures; and it can lead to biases in interpreting known facts. Both great fear and great anger can do this. People who are very frightened or very angry will often be incapable of taking in what is said to them; they remember incidents which justify the emotion they feel, and they become incapable of seeing inconsistencies in their own beliefs, particularly those about the object of their fear or anger. They resort to stereotyped forms of thinking and ritualised ways of seeing the world.

The effects of anger upon cognition clearly have implications for how the emotion should be handled when manifested in any extreme form, since rational argument or appeals to good judgement will have limited effect. One technique which is commonly used by psychologists is to deal with the underlying level of arousal rather than the emotion in which it is crystallised. This involves a sort of 'time out'. The person exhibiting an excessive level of arousal is isolated and given time to return to a lower level. Obviously, this is only possible when the practitioner has some control over the environment and there is space for the time out. In the field, practitioners use other 'cool-down' tactics that serve the same purpose. They may refuse to continue an interview until the client calms down; they may break the exchange by sending the client into the kitchen to make tea; they may, with younger clients, request them to leave the room for several minutes; and so on. All of these tactics share a common assumption – that reasoning with someone who is highly excited is pointless. The objective is to reduce the overall level of arousal and then deal with the reasons for it arising.

PRACTITIONER VIOLENCE

So far, it has been implicit that violence and powerful emotions are the preserve of the recipients of care. This is clearly nonsense. Practitioners can become angry and violent in the course of their work. They too are susceptible to frustration and they also have personal goals they seek to achieve in their relationships with clients. Practitioners sometimes test and incite their charges. In discussions of violence in the caring professions this issue is rarely addressed.

There is no really hard evidence on practitioner violence towards clients. The assertion that it exists is based upon anecdotal reports. Yet the frequency of these is enough to give rise to concern, even if most of the incidents involve very minor violence. Examples arise from all sectors of the caring professions, especially those where the clients involved are particularly powerless. For instance, a nurse reported how bath time on her geriatric ward was the point in the day when tempers often frayed and she found herself becoming unnecessarily rough with the elderly confused patients she was handling. Residential social workers in a hostel for adolescent boys explained that they had to use violence to establish their authority and create an identity for themselves. A teacher described how one day she became furious with a lad in the fourth year who was disturbing her class, she grabbed him and shook him until she heard his teeth chatter. These examples reflect only the most visible aspect of practitioner violence – that which practitioners are willing to report freely when questioned. Perhaps the more covert forms will only become acknowledged when clients, patients or pupils are asked about this problem by independent researchers.

It is important to bear in mind that clients, pupils and patients may have a very different perspective on the activities of their carers. Actions which carers themselves regard as perfectly routine, necessary and unexceptional may be seen as aggressive or violent by the client, pupil or patient. For instance, the teacher who embarrasses a child in order to emphasise a point may consider the tactic normal, while the child may see it as a direct attack. The teacher who throws chalk at and hits an inattentive child may feel the approach has a venerable tradition, but the child may see it as a direct attack. The social worker who challenges a woman's ability to look after her child may think she is doing her job in protecting the baby, the mother may consider it an unnecessary insult. The doctor who slaps a patient who is hysterical may see it as acceptable, the man slapped may view it as an attack. These cases may seem obvious. The disparity in labelling the acts as violent are based on different understandings of what role the carer occupies and what rights that role allots. But the importance of the client's perspective should not be ignored. How the client defines your activities dictates how he or she responds. Also, there are some situations where the meaning and nature of a carer's actions are genuinely unclear. Who is the aggressor in the following scenario?

> *A couple arrive at an accident department of a hospital. They are arguing. The man is dishevelled and bleeding from cuts about his face and arms. The woman is calling him a fool and telling him that he is no 'man'. He pushes her away. She starts to pummel his chest. A young doctor steps in to pull her away, catching her wrists and accidentally twisting them. She cries out in pain. The man immediately grabs the doctor telling him to leave his wife. The doctor struggles to get loose. Lashing out, he kicks the man who crumples on the ground.*

Depending on your point of view, there is a case to be made for each of the three protagonists in this scene to be considered the aggressor. This illustrates that violence is a process. It is a process of interaction between people, and frequently people do what is dictated by a complex pattern of circumstances, at a particular moment, in a particular situation. Practitioner violence may be a reality, but it will be contingent upon a complex interaction of factors at the time it occurs. It is not simply restricted to a few 'bad' practitioners who are in some way aberrant. It is a realistic possibility for anyone.

The existence of practitioner violence serves to emphasise the mutuality of the emotions which arise in the caring relationship. The practitioner is not segregated from the problems of his or her client. The practitioner is emotionally at risk in any caring relationship, but obviously in some more than others. Some of the caring professions advocate the use of the practitioner's own emotional resources to a greater extent than others. There seems to be an inverse relationship between the amount of emotional involvement required and the degree to which there is a scientific basis for the interventions of the profession. The greater the emotional involvement of the practitioner, the greater the stress he or she will experience.

STRESS AND VIOLENCE

There is an interesting relationship between violence and stress. In so far as stress is both a product of unpleasant experiences and a form of unpleasant experience in itself, it may be both the cause and the result of violence. Some aspects of the nature and effects of stress will now be described, followed by an examination of how stress relates to the reasons why practitioners may become violent, and how it may affect the ways in which they can deal with violence from others. It is also useful to understand something of stress reactions when considering why clients or patients become violent.

WHAT CAUSES STRESS?

Anyone will become stressed when the external demands that they have to satisfy outstrip their personal resources – in retailing terms when demand exceeds supply. People have different personal resources (e.g. intelligence, physical strength, self-confidence or knowledge) and possess them in various degrees. This means that we each meet the demands of our work, family or community with a different set of skills or capacities. Demands which would outstrip the resources of one person will not unduly bother the next.

We know, however, what sorts of thing tend to induce stress for most people, including members of the caring professions. Major life events such as bereavement, divorce or moving house cause stress. Events that would typically be regarded as pleasant, like marriage or the birth of a child can also be stressful for some people. Any big changes, nasty or nice, make demands and are potential sources of stress.

People become distressed when they have to adjust to change. Even relatively small changes can generate stress, especially if they are very rapid. The major sources of stress at work have been extensively studied. The top ten for the caring professions can be listed:

1. Long or unsociable hours which destroy home life.

2. Job insecurity, especially worries about management reorganisation or changes in job specification.

3. Not knowing what standards of service provision you can realistically be expected to achieve.

4. Poor pay or promotion prospects.

5. Lack of autonomy or ability to participate in decision making.

6. Work overload: either too much or the wrong sort.

7. Poor relationships with other colleagues, so that they fail to support you.

THE STRESS CHECKLIST

The Stress Checklist is designed to give you some idea of how stressed you are at work. Put a tick in the column which best reflects what is true for you. Go through the list quickly, without spending too long considering each question – your first response is normally the most revealing. Be honest; after all, only you will see the results.

	Always	Sometimes	Rarely	Never
1. I finish the working day feeling satisfied with what I've done.				
2. I feel in control of my life.				
3. I experience dizzy spells or palpitations.				
4. I feel tiredness or lack of energy.				
5. I have difficulty getting to sleep.				
6. I am confident about the future.				
7. I have a poor appetite.				
8. I lose my temper over small things.				
9. I can rely on my family or friends to support me if I need help.				
10. I find the amount of work I have exceeds the amount of time available for it.				
11. I feel I'm as good as anyone else at the job I do.				
12. I find my management supportive.				
13. I look forward to going to work.				
14. I do not know what I'm working for.				
15. I am unable to unwind in the evening.				
16. I have more responsibility than I can handle.				
17. I drink too much alcohol.				
18. I can switch off thinking about problems.				
19. I think I manage my time well.				
20. I know how to refuse to take on additional work if I need to.				

Stress Checklist Scoring

▶ Questions 1, 2, 6, 9, 11, 12, 13, 18, 19, 20: Score 1 for 'Always', 2 for 'Sometimes', 3 for 'Rarely', and 4 for 'Never'.

▶ Questions 3, 4, 5, 7, 8, 10, 14, 15, 16, 17: Score 4 for 'Always', 3 for 'Sometimes', 2 for 'Rarely', and 1 for 'Never'.

Maximum score 80
Minimum score 20

Interpretation of Checklist Scores

Interpretation of the scores needs to be done with some caution. Two people with the same overall score may react differently for a number of reasons: the sources of the stress may be different and the strategies they adopt to cope with it may be different. These interpretations are meant as guidelines which enable you to compare yourself with others.

Score

70–80   Very few people experience this level of stress. The level of stress with which you are dealing is very high and you should take some action to remove yourself from the source of the stress.

60–70   About 20% of the working population experience this level of stress. Some remedial action is advisable. The longer you bear this level of stress, the more difficult things will tend to become.

40–60   Scores in this range represent a moderate normal level of stress for a busy professional. You should monitor yourself for any drift towards greater levels and watch especially for particular periods or events when stress increases sharply.

20–40   Enviably low level of stress. (Did you answer all the questions honestly?)

It is worth keeping a note of your stress score and rechecking your stress level at regular intervals, or after significant changes in your lifestyle (such as marriage, birth of a child, move of house), or job description (such as promotion, change of department or region of operation, move to a new employer). Changes can occur without us noticing until the effects are serious because the psychological and physical consequences of stress are gradual and cumulative.

Once you have determined your stress score, you might wish to compare it with the scores of colleagues. This can be instructive because you might be able to pinpoint common sources of stress which stem from working in the caring professions. Then you could consider together what changes need to be introduced.

8. Ineffective or time-wasting arrangements for dealing with clients or patients.

9. Poor communication channels, either with managers or with clients or patients, which make it difficult to do the work.

10. Boredom. Paradoxical creatures that we are, we dislike change *and* the absence of change. Repetition of the same job over a long period results in increased errors of judgement and a general deterioration of performance.

WHAT ARE THE EFFECTS OF STRESS?

Stressors arouse your system, an effect known as the General Adaptation Syndrome (GAS). Basically, we become alarmed when faced with a stressor and the body readies itself for 'flight or fight'. Adrenalin levels rise, blood pressure increases, respiration rate alters, and we are ready to outrun or outgun an attacker. Neither response is particularly useful when the stressors are not of the variety which can be evaded or frightened off. Most stressors nowadays are complex and long term, embedded in the nature of the job. The body's anachronistic response, which may have been functional when facing simple, acute dangers in the past, becomes a hazard in itself. When all activity fails to remove the stressor, exhaustion results and is manifested at a number of levels.

PSYCHOLOGICAL EFFECTS

1. *Thinking decrements*: memory deteriorates, distractibility increases, concentration and attention span decline, powers of organisation and long-term planning crumble.

2. *Emotional changes*: hostility and defensiveness increase, depression sets in, feelings of powerlessness and worthlessness appear, cynicism about the motives and value of others grows, mood swings (from sadness to happiness, optimism to pessimism) become more sudden and frequent, hypochondria becomes evident, and personality changes can occur (for instance, neat people become untidy or vice versa).

BEHAVIOURAL EFFECTS

Stress can have many different specific effects upon behaviour, but some occur frequently. Enthusiasms disappear, once cherished hobbies are abandoned. Energy levels are lowered so that everything seems to be too much trouble. Sleep is disrupted because it is difficult to get to sleep and then to wake up. Drinking can increase, so can smoking. Absenteeism from work is common. People's sex drive is often reduced.

STRESS AND THE CARING PROFESSIONS

Members of the caring professions are prime candidates for high stress levels. In virtually all cases, it is as if their job descriptions had been written specifically to *encourage* stress. Even when people choose to do the job and are aware of the stress they will face, the pressures have an effect eventually. Examples of colleagues who have suffered 'burnout' will be familiar to anybody in the caring professions. Burnout is just a catchy label for the stress syndrome. It does, however, illustrate one result of stress in the context of caring: burnout is associated with a growing disinterest in the welfare of the client and a desire to withdraw from clients. This decline in 'care' about the client is interesting in the light of the relationship between stress and practitioner violence.

Stress has two main effects upon the practitioner's involvement in violent incidents:

1. Increased stress, especially if very rapid, will increase the overall likelihood that the practitioner will commit some violent act because of the emotional instability and deterioration in self-control which stress tends to produce.

2. Increased stress will decrease the practitioner's chances of anticipating or handling violence from a client successfully, since it tends to reduce cognitive efficiency and emotional control.

The implication is that if you want to control both your own tendency to violence and that of your clients, it is important first to find ways of minimising the impact of stress.

COPING WITH STRESS

There are no easy remedies for stress. But there are three useful points to remember when dealing with it.

1. Monitor your own stress level. It is all too easy to be overwhelmed by a gradual increase in sources of stress over a long period. Do not

dismiss it when someone close to you suggests you are changing or showing signs of stress. Take stock; decide for yourself whether you feel you are coping well. Remember: people thrive at different levels of stress. You may be able to tolerate more than most, but be aware of where the limits are. You will know then when to draw back from the brink. Use The Stress Checklist to estimate your own stress level.

2. If you feel stressed at work identify the source. It may lie in yourself (for instance if you are too ready to accept more work); it may lie in the nature of the company or the structure of the management (most of the sources of stress at work listed earlier could be said at one level to be the products of bad management). Try to locate the real origin of your sense of distress and set about changing that. One of the symptoms of excess stress is the victim's inability to analyse what is generating the problem. If you have trouble in identifying the source of the stress seek help. Often friends or family can see what is just too close to your nose for you to recognise yourself. At work, if you seek help from colleagues you may well find that problems that you think are purely personal turn out to be shared by your colleagues. Recognising this will stop you blaming yourself for being unable to cope. Succumbing to stress is rarely a result of personal inadequacy.

3. Sometimes you are unable to change the source of your stress. If this is your predicament, there are two options.

   You could escape: retreat in the face of such a stress is not defeat, and there will be many other types of work which you can do. Too often people think that they can do nothing other than their current job, even when doing it is distressing them. You have to do a cost–benefit analysis and decide whether changing job is more costly than staying where you are.

   Alternatively you could fight the symptoms of stress in yourself, and learn how to handle high levels of stress. Some of the best methods of stress damage limitation involve introducing more organisation into your day. Plan the day in advance and build into your schedule two short breaks (of about 10–15 minutes) mid-morning and afternoon when you can be alone and quiet (this can be done in the car on the road to a visit, or in an unused interview room, or in an empty classroom at break). During this time try not to think about the problems of work. Think instead about some pleasant event or experience or clear your mind altogether. Relax your body, breathe evenly and slowly. Make these breaks a routine and after a few days you will probably feel noticeably less tired at the end of the day. Combine these breaks with careful consideration of your diet (do not eat on the run, eat 'healthy' foods, eat at regular times, etc.). These relatively simple tactics are believed by many psychologists to be effective in relieving stress. In arming yourself against stress, you are also indirectly arming against violence.

Chapter Three

Common Features of Attacks and Explanations of Violence

There are serious problems for anyone trying to give estimates of the frequency with which carers face aggression and violence. Firstly, there are very few comprehensive surveys. The majority of studies which have examined rates and forms of assault have been restricted to a single professional group and have involved relatively small geographical areas (a single county for example). In summarising the information available on incidence rates, it is therefore necessary to build up a picture of what happens from a lot of different pockets of data.

Secondly, the definitions of aggression and violence differ across studies. One study will examine only physical assault which has led to injury, another will include everything from verbal abuse onwards. This means that information from different studies can only be compared with great caution.

Studies also differ in the methods adopted to collect information. Some rely on administrative records of reported incidents; others employ interviews with random or specific samples of practitioners; and others use large-scale questionnaire surveys. The important thing to note is that different data collection methods give rise to differing conclusions about rates of violence. It is not entirely evident which estimates are most valid. A range of studies is described below, and each study gives a different perspective on the form and frequency of assaults experienced by practitioners. Taken together they provide a useful framework for comparison in assessing your personal experiences.

VIOLENCE IN THE HEALTH SERVICES

Perhaps the most comprehensive study of violence in the health services was conducted in 1986 by the Health and Safety Commission. It comprised a survey of 5,000 health workers (1,000 in each of five District Health Authorities: Newcastle, Exeter, Croydon, Fife, and Birmingham), of whom 3,000 ultimately responded to the enquiry. The Commission's report *Violence to Staff in the Health Services* defined four categories of violence:

- injury requiring medical assistance
- injury requiring first aid
- involving threat with a weapon
- involving verbal abuse.

The survey showed that 1 in 200 workers had suffered a major injury following a violent attack during the preceding year. A further 1 in 10 needed first aid and 1 in 20 had been threatened with knives, chairs, broken bottles, and the like. As many as 1 in 6 had been threatened verbally. These estimates are based on a 60 per cent response to the survey. It may be that they overestimate the incidence rate if those who responded were more likely to have been involved in violent incidents. This is always a difficulty with postal surveys: you never know what those who do not respond would have said. Nevertheless, a 60 per cent response is normally regarded as a respectable basis for generalisation in survey research.

The Health and Safety Commission figures can be compared with rates of personal violence generally. A Home Office study (1984) of incidents of personal violence reported to the police forces showed the incidence rate for serious wounding to be 1 in 5,300 for males and 1 in 25,000 for females. For less serious wounding the rates were 1 in 310 and 1 in 880 respectively. Police statistics may underestimate the rate of personal violence, since not all incidents are reported, but if these official figures are taken seriously, it seems that health service workers are at least 26 times more likely to be seriously injured than the general public. The increased risk is greater for female health workers. The general figures may be considered an inappropriate basis for comparison since they are gross estimates, but even when other comparators are chosen the picture looks unhealthy. The rate of serious injury in the health service is twice as high as in the construction industry and five times as high as in the manufacturing sector.

It is also useful to compare these figures with the incidence rates of violence for the police force. In the *Police Review* for April 1987, 28 out of 43 forces were able to provide figures on violence to police personnel. There were 9,954 reported assaults in 1986 for 82,043 personnel (a rate of about 1 in 8). Seventeen of the forces responding were able to say that 22,907 days' work were lost due to assaults. That means 70,000 days if extrapolated to all forces, representing a cost of 3·5 million pounds per year. These figures are not atypical for the previous five years.

There is a limited amount of regional variation in violence rates. South Wales was top of the league with 1 in 4·2 assaulted; Avon and Somerset had 1 in 5·2; the West Midlands had 1 in 5·5; and the Metropolitan force had 1 in 7·9. The comparability across forces is however dubious due to different recording systems. These are also the most conservative estimates of rates of assault since many go unreported. Furthermore, many members of the force are not involved in direct contact with the public but the figures are based on total personnel; this suggests that the field force is more at risk than the incidence rates imply.

The problem with reporting rates applies to the health services as well. The Health Service Advisory Committee claims that at least one third of serious incidents in the health services goes unreported.

According to the Health and Safety Commission's study, most types of serious incident were more frequent in psychiatric facilities. In such settings, 1 in 4 respondents had suffered minor injury after attacks. In geriatric and psychiatric hospitals the comparable figure was 1 in 5. The staff who are most vulnerable across settings are student nurses and ambulance drivers. Interestingly, given what was said earlier about frustration and pain as a cause of violence, the places where most attacks take place are hospital emergency and accident departments.

These findings have been supported by other studies. The National Association of Health Authorities in 1987 found that one in three District Health Authorities had experienced increased rates of assault upon their staff. (The actual number had risen by up to 47 per cent over the preceding three-year period.) The victims in these assaults were primarily nurses, their attackers were frequently drunk or on drugs, and the incidents took place late at night in emergency or accident departments.

As a result of their research, the Health Services Advisory Committee recommended:

1. Using physical devices to offer protection (personal alarms, panic buttons, two-way radios). (The Royal College of Nursing suggested installing video cameras in dangerous departments.)

2. Redesigning reception areas and waiting rooms to make them less isolated and more homely.

3. Minimising delays and telling people why they have to wait if they do – perhaps by providing simple explanatory leaflets.

4. Providing adequate and flexible staffing levels to ensure that individuals are not isolated for long periods.

5. Providing training courses in prevention and management of violence, including self-confidence and assertiveness courses together with the traditional self-defence techniques (only 12 per cent of staff in the sample reported having previously had any training).

6. Offering support and counselling to victims and information on the legal assistance and compensation available.

7. Improving the flow of information about and to patients (especially where changes have occurred, for instance when new staff take over or new patients arrive, or if there has been a change in mental or physical state of the patient, or if a history of violence is known to exist).

8. A detailed plan should be kept centrally of staff whereabouts during domiciliary or community visits. Procedural guidelines should be laid out for dealing with potential or actual violence. Information should be provided for all staff on high-risk areas (for example particular parts of the town or city) and on high-risk patients. Extra precautions should be taken, especially by female staff, at night. Where risks are high, home visits should be avoided and interviews transferred to an office. Doctors in several areas have acted on this advice and have abandoned night calls.

9. Increased liaison with police, either where violence is anticipated or in reporting it after the event.

10. Maintaining sufficient staffing levels. Overtime and long hours should be reduced, since tired staff may be less able to cope with potential violence. More flexible appointments would make it possible to switch staff around, spreading the amount of hours worked more evenly. Extra cover should be provided for nights, weekends and shift changeovers. Individuals, especially if junior, should not be isolated for long periods and backup should be readily available if an incident occurs. If the existence of a risk is established, appropriate staffing should be agreed and maintained.

11. Efficient and accurate recording of incidents in order to provide an

adequate basis for the immediate response to the incident and for longer-term strategic planning.

These recommendations are reasonably typical of one school of thought about the way in which violence must be contained. The changes suggested are largely administrative or organisational, with new systems being introduced which will then facilitate changes in the way individuals can operate.

VIOLENCE IN THE SOCIAL SERVICES

Probably the most comprehensive research on violence against social workers was conducted by Rowett (1986), using an integrated methods approach. The research had three layers: a postal survey of all 132 local authorities (68,000 social workers were contacted, 40 per cent of whom responded); a postal survey of all social workers in one shire county (728 employees were approached and 450 returned usable questionnaires); and an in-depth interview study of 120 of the social workers who had returned questionnaires. Respondents were asked about incidents of physical assault which had led to actual physical harm. Other forms of assault were not included.

The national survey of social services departments showed an annual average rate of 1 assault for 259 posts, which amounts to 90 assaults per year. It should be noted that this rate was increasing over a five-year period: 43 assaults in 1978 compared with 132 in 1982. For shire counties the rate was 1 assault to 434 staff. For metropolitan districts it was 1 to 130. There was a disparity in the rates for fieldworkers and residential workers: for fieldworkers it was 1:372; for residential workers it was 1:228.

The questionnaire from social workers in the social services department of one shire county showed that 25 per cent of them had been attacked over a five-year period from 1978–82. This should be compared with the predicted 2 per cent from Rowett's national survey, which emphasises the inadequacy of official recording of violent incidents. The injuries reported varied in severity: 76 per cent were 'minor', 28 per cent 'moderately serious', and 6 per cent 'severe'. It seems likely that the minor injuries go unreported and therefore never appear in any official statistics. This survey confirmed the national picture in that residential workers were more at risk than fieldworkers: 66 per cent of reported assaults were on residential staff. The survey also showed another interesting feature of these assaults. As many as 85 per cent of them were committed by established clients whom the social worker had known for some time; a further 10 per cent were members of a client's family.

Detailed interviews were conducted with a subsample of those who returned questionnaires. Sixty social workers who reported assaults were paired with 60 who had no history of assault. The samples were split evenly between residential and fieldworkers and almost equally by sex. The assaulted and non-assaulted samples were matched for age, grade, length of experience, geographical area of work and qualifications. The 20 male residential workers had experienced between them 189 assaults leading to physical injury; the ten female residential workers had experienced 313. The rates for the fieldworkers were lower: 69 for the 15 men and 17 for the 15 women.

Information was collected on the characteristics of the assailants, the situational factors that the victim considered important to the attack, the social worker's response to the attack, and the personal characteristics of the victim. In addition there was a serious attempt to assess the beliefs which both the assaulted and non-assaulted social workers held about the typical assailant, the types of situation in which violence occurs and types of violence involved, the most appropriate responses to attack, and the sort of person who gets attacked.

Before reading the results of this part of the research, you may want to record your own beliefs about these features of the violent incident by completing the self-assessment exercise on pages 34–35.

CHARACTERISTICS OF THE ASSAILANT
Rowett did find that assailants could be characterised. Sixty per cent of the assaults on residential workers and 30 per cent of the assaults on fieldworkers were committed by clients under the age of 18. This perhaps reflects the relative proportion of clients which the two branches of social work have in this age category. Residential workers tended to be assaulted by males. Fieldworkers were mostly assaulted by females. No female fieldworker in this sample was assaulted by a man.

The assailants were all classified as coming from socio-economic classes IV or V. (This fact, however, is likely to be meaningless, since it merely reflects the disparity in the frequencies with which the different classes use the social services.

Of the 60 social workers assaulted, eight were attacked by a client who was mentally ill. In fact, 38 per cent of the assailants had a history

FEATURES OF ATTACKS

Simply record your answers to the questions below and then compare them with what you subsequently learn from the research which is summarised. Check whether your beliefs parallel those of other practitioners.

1. Rate practitioners who get assaulted by clients on the following characteristics:

	Extremely	Very	Quite	Not much	Not at all
Liberal	☐	☐	☐	☐	☐
Dogmatic	☐	☐	☐	☐	☐
Authoritarian	☐	☐	☐	☐	☐
Gentle	☐	☐	☐	☐	☐
Provocative	☐	☐	☐	☐	☐
Strong	☐	☐	☐	☐	☐
Willing to take risks	☐	☐	☐	☐	☐
Experienced	☐	☐	☐	☐	☐
Competent	☐	☐	☐	☐	☐
Insightful	☐	☐	☐	☐	☐

2. Rank the following types of violence according to their likelihood of occurrence in practice: pushing; hair pulling; verbal abuse; sexual abuse; holding; damage to personal property; stabbing; strangulation; sexual assault; punching; and kicking.

3. Rank the following contexts according to the likelihood that assaults will take place in them: the assailant's home; the practitioner's car; the practitioner's office; communal areas in an institution; bathrooms in an institution; on the street.

4. Rate the likelihood of the following types of client or patient being involved in an assault:

	Not at all	*Quite low*	*Sometimes*	*Quite high*	*Very high*
Elderly mentally ill	☐	☐	☐	☐	☐
Parent of children being taken into care	☐	☐	☐	☐	☐
Mentally handicapped	☐	☐	☐	☐	☐
Those with a history of psychiatric illness	☐	☐	☐	☐	☐
Those in socio-economic classes I and II	☐	☐	☐	☐	☐
Those with a criminal conviction	☐	☐	☐	☐	☐
Children in residential care	☐	☐	☐	☐	☐
Those who are drunk	☐	☐	☐	☐	☐
Those in extreme pain	☐	☐	☐	☐	☐
New clients or patients	☐	☐	☐	☐	☐

of one or more psychiatric admissions. Forty-five per cent had been convicted of at least one criminal offence and 28 per cent had convictions for violence. Ninety-two per cent had undergone recent stressful events in their lives. This confirms that stress needs to be taken seriously as a predictor of violence.

Social workers were asked to say who they would expect to be the most and least likely aggressors across client groups. They felt the most likely would be parents of children who were being taken into care, the mentally ill in the community and children in residential care. They expected the mentally handicapped in the community and the elderly in care to be the least likely to be violent. These beliefs do seem to be borne out by the actual incidence rates, though it is difficult to know how far they themselves shape what people are willing to report about violent incidents.

CONTEXT OF THE ASSAULT

Echoing the findings of Rowett's national survey, assaults never occurred on first contact with the social worker. In 47 per cent of cases, the social worker attacked rated the relationship with the assailant as good before the attack. Attacks tended to take place in the client's primary or secondary territory (which means in the home, or in the cases of institutionalised clients in areas where they feel some sense of possession or control). The physical assault was almost always preceded by verbal abuse or threats.

When asked what they believed to be the most frequent places in which violence occurred, assaulted and non-assaulted alike stated that they believed that violence was most likely in the client's home and in the social services offices. The first belief is supported by the evidence, the second is not.

TYPES OF VIOLENCE

Interviewees indicated what they thought to be the most likely types of violence they would have to face. The rank ordering from most likely to least was: pushing, holding, kicking, punching, hair pulling, stabbing, strangulation. None considered sexual assault likely. Again there were no differences between those social workers who had been assaulted and those who had not.

CHARACTERISTICS OF ASSAULTED SOCIAL WORKERS

All the interviewees seemed to believe that social workers who were assaulted were more provocative, incompetent, authoritarian and inexperienced. They were felt to seek out risky situations, confront clients and challenge them unnecessarily. They were thought to be more demanding, less flexible and less able to detect potentially dangerous situations. It is interesting that the assaulted shared this set of beliefs about the characteristics typifying other victims of attack. This must be compared with their equally forcefully expressed belief that their own assaults were never purely their own fault.

It is notable in the light of this stereotype of the assaulted social worker that when interviewees completed a test designed to measure hostility levels all fell within the normal range and there were no differences between residential or field workers or between assaulted and non-assaulted. There seems little firm evidence for this pervasive stereotype.

There was some belief that sex and physique were predisposing factors for assault. However, there was no consistent pattern in the attitudes expressed: some considered women to be more at risk, others thought men more open to attack; some thought small stature an incitement to attack, others felt the big and strong were fairer game. Again there is no real evidence to support these beliefs.

Issues surrounding the stereotyping of the assaulted practitioner are addressed further in Chapter 5, but it is worth noting here that the stereotype is damningly negative and might be expected to affect the way a victim of attack can handle the experience. It may go some way to accounting for failure to report incidents (20 per cent in Rowett's sample had not reported attacks). It may also account for some of the reluctance on the part of managers to provide support for victims (which happened in one third of cases reported), who are seen in part as the originators of their own problem.

It would be inappropriate to rely solely on Rowett's research for the picture of violence in the social services. There have been other influential studies; these tend to be smaller scale and based in a single geographical region, but often they have led to recommendations specifically tailored for an authority willing to implement them. A small sample of these will be described just to give the reader the feel for their findings after a brief description of the only other relevant national survey.

The Labour Research Department in July 1987 reported on a

survey of 210 workplaces as part of their *Bargaining Report*. These 210 workplaces included 46 social services offices spread across the country. Of the social services offices surveyed, 96 per cent reported some experience of verbal abuse in the office during a two-month period, 93 per cent had threats of violence, 67 per cent had threats backed with a weapon, 83 per cent had actual violence, 41 per cent had violence with a weapon. Respondents perceived violence to be increasing in these offices and claimed it was caused by reductions in staffing and increases in client frustration due to increased unemployment. Half considered greater general public frustration to be the cause. Only a minority of workplaces reported any systematic monitoring of violent incidents. A number of factooors were felt to place staff at risk – 91 per cent identified lack of training, 87 per cent working in isolation, 74 per cent staff shortages, 63 per cent inadequate security. Any anti-violence measures taken in workplaces tended to follow union pressure (11 per cent had taken industrial action to protest about attacks on staff). In general, the report supports the idea that workers are demanding that employers take more responsibility for safety.

❏ After industrial action by its staff in protest against the frequency of attacks, Strathclyde Regional Council conducted a survey during late 1985, recording any act of violence in all of its social work locations. The definition of violence adopted included verbal intimidation: 'violence is a purposeful or reactive behaviour intending to produce damaging or hurtful effects, physically or emotionally on other persons'. In an eight-week period, 16 fieldwork teams reported seven attacks (five in the social services office). Two assessment centres accounted for 21 of the total of 76 violent acts reported and eight children's homes for 30 more. The violence occurred mainly when social workers intervened to stop a fight or to impose rules for inmates' behaviour. Strathclyde produced a series of recommendations about how violence could be contained. These are discussed in Chapter 4.

❏ Also in 1985, Leeds Social Services Department found that there were 200 violent incidents in 109 establishments over a four-week period. The worst affected locations were old people's homes and adolescent treatment centres. Most incidents occurred in communal areas at times when the officer in charge was off duty. Only 86 of the 200 incidents were officially recorded. And 177 were repeat incidents, attributed to the inappropriate placement of clients. The Leeds report called for staff training in causes of conflict, methods of safe physical restraint, and techniques for disarming an attacker.

❏ Surrey County Council Social Services Department conducted its survey in 1987 and the findings are reported in *Safe and Secure in Surrey?* The survey covered all 4,000 plus employees in the county using a postal questionnaire. In total, 1,570 responded. Of these, 528 had experience of some sort of violence: 208 of physical assault, 261 of physical abuse, 4 of sexual assault, 59 of sexual abuse, 327 of verbal threat, and 108 of property damage or theft. This means that roughly 1 in 3 employees who responded had reported some sort of violence.

The study showed that social workers were most vulnerable in their cars, then in clients' homes, and then in social work offices. Few had received training in handling violence. Line managers were much criticised for not taking appropriate action and particularly for not changing practices as a result of incidents.

The Surrey survey serves to emphasise the extent of the experience of violence, where workers are most vulnerable and what types of professional task lead most readily to violence.

Recommendations from the Surrey study highlighted the need for more informed placement decisions which take account of the worker's experience and qualifications; the desirability of bringing about a reduction in client waiting time to see workers; the advantages of an organisational culture where worries can be expressed so that risks can be anticipated; and the value of spreading staff across duty times so that a full range of skills is available to be called upon most of the time. The need for good information on clients was emphasised – biographical information will predict tendencies to violence. It was notable that workers underplay the seriousness of the threats they face. This may be an effective way of handling the build-up of anxiety but it hampers accurate prediction of incidents. It was certainly true that workers were most vulnerable on duty, when taking a child into care and when involved in compulsorily admitting someone to a psychiatric hospital.

HOMES FOR THE ELDERLY
Given that the elderly are believed by social workers to be one of the least violent client groups, it is perhaps useful to conclude this section with some evidence on them.

❏ Hampshire Social Services conducted a survey of violence in their homes for the elderly in 1984. Violence was defined as 'aggressive behaviour resulting in physical contact'. Fifty-five out of 62 local authority homes for the elderly responded to the survey's questionnaire.

Twenty-six reported violent incidents in the six-month period January–June 1984; these were mostly minor in nature. Four homes for the elderly mentally ill reported a high frequency of violent incidents but only two were considered in the main report because the others could not give sufficient details on incidents.

Forty-six non-specialist homes reported 59 incidents (21 of which were by residents against staff, half in residents' bedrooms; and 38 of which were by residents against other residents, mostly in the lounge area). This yields an actual incidence rate of 2·1 per home in six months if those reporting no incidents are excluded. The two homes for the elderly mentally ill reported 64 incidents between them (38 resident to staff; 26 resident to resident). This is probably an underestimate since not all incidents are recorded nor is recording systematic.

Recording of causes for incidents was poor: but confusion, senile dementia or mental disorder were frequent causes; so too was resistance to staff attention or handling. In the case of resident to resident aggression, intolerance of psychogeriatrics, argument and confusion seemed major causes. It became apparent that some patients were repeat offenders. It is possible that this may be due to inappropriate placements. New residents also seemed to provide particular problems; again this may be due to initial mis-assessments which were subsequently corrected. Audiovisual handicaps lead to misunderstanding and suspicion which often become expressed in physical violence. Lack of space and privacy were also identified as major triggers for violence.

It therefore seems that while the elderly as a client group are less violent, there is some risk of violence; particularly when they are mentally ill.

VIOLENCE IN SCHOOLS

❏ In 1986, the National Association of Schoolmasters and Union of Women Teachers published their report of a survey of teachers *Pupil Violence and Serious Disorder in Schools*. In it they report that one in five teachers had experienced pupil violence resulting in serious injury on one or more occasions in a six-month period between September 1984 and February 1985. One in four had been threatened with violence. One in ten had suffered an attempted attack. One in twenty-five had suffered actual physical violence.

At first sight this seems to reflect an ongoing war in our schools. The reality may not be quite as grim. Findings were based on a survey of

125,000 teachers, but only 3,910 of these replied. This is equivalent to a five per cent return rate which most social researchers would consider an inadequate basis for any conclusions. It is likely that those most motivated to respond would be those most concerned with violence in schools – those involved in it. It is, however, worth presenting the results of this survey together with the word of caution about generalising from them. The survey has been influential in the popular debate about violence in our schools and such evidence is changing general attitudes about the state of education and is designed to affect policy making.

❏ The criticism concerning low and potentially biased return rates cannot be levelled at a more recent study conducted by National Opinion Polls for the National Union of Teachers (NUT). They used a representative sample of teachers from state and independent schools. Out of the 1,000 approached, 484 returned their postal questionnaire. Fifty per cent of these said indiscipline was a frequent or regular occurrence in the classroom. One in three had experienced a major disruption in class in the last year. One in five reported physical violence, though not always directed at themselves. Nevertheless, it should be added that one in ten thought classroom behaviour to be 'no problem'. This study, like several others conducted in schools, makes it clear that the day-to-day disruption of classes is more important to teachers than the rare cases of actual violence.

❏ Indiscipline is seen to be a growing problem. The National Association of Head Teachers conducted a poll of its members and found that 16 per cent thought indiscipline to be a regular problem and 28 per cent thought it frequent. Fifty per cent of those who had been in the same school for five years felt that the problem had become worse during that time, 18 per cent said that pupils had attacked teachers in their schools, 3 per cent reported that parents had been violent to teachers, 25 per cent had received verbal abuse from children and 8 per cent from their parents.

Houghton and colleagues (1988) claim violence itself is not the main problem in schools. High frequency non-violent behaviour is the problem. This mainly involves pupils talking out of turn and disrupting the class so that teachers cannot structure lessons effectively. This conclusion concurs with the NUT study, and is based on a survey of a random sample of teachers in six secondary schools in one West Midlands local education authority. Over 60 per cent of those approached completed the questionnaire. Respondents were completely anonymous so as to liberate them to tell of incidents without fear of any personal consequences. Fifty-five per cent found themselves spending too much time on problems of order and control. Fifty per cent found talking out of turn to be the most troublesome behaviour; 17 per cent cited hindering other children as a serious problem too. Only two teachers cited physical aggression as troublesome.

The study by Wheldall and Merrett would seem to minimise the role of violence in classrooms. This may however be a consequence of the question which they asked, which concerned 'troublesome' behaviour. Violence may not be troublesome, it may be something more than that. It may be frightening or worrying or destructive.

It is certainly seen to be a real concern by the Professional Association of Teachers. It has declared that highly disruptive pupils should be allowed to leave school at 15 and the money saved should be spent on better nursery education to improve the next generation of secondary school pupils.

Across the board, groups representing the views of teachers are calling for some strategy to cope with the declining standards of discipline they perceive in schools. There have been calls for the media to be marshalled to promote good behaviour through modelling and vicarious reinforcement. There have been suggestions that parents who do not control their children should take responsibility for covering the costs of the damage they cause. There is the inevitable demand that teachers should be trained to deal with discipline and this is tied to the argument that teacher trainers should have to spend much more time at the sharp end of education, teaching in schools, so that they do not become insulated from the problems facing new teachers. There is a notion that there should be more 'special units' (or, more colloquially, 'sin bins') where particularly troublesome pupils can be isolated and taught by highly-paid staff with great experience in handling problems. There is the even more politically charged possibility that local education authorities will have the final decision on whether to expel or suspend a pupil taken out of their hands.

Initially, it is rather difficult to compare the violence teachers may face with that experienced by other professionals. Evidence of the psychological or social profiles of pupil attackers is not available in the surveys quoted. Nor is information on the specific context or background to attacks available. Without this, effective comparisons are impossible. These two areas do require urgent attention. It is only when this information is available that the viability of any recommendations for change in the education system can be evaluated.

INCIDENCE AND FEATURES OF ATTACKS: SOME CONCLUSIONS

There is now considerable information available on the incidence rates of violence in the health and social services and, increasingly, in the education services. The trouble is that there is no consistency in the definitions of violence, the techniques for sampling or the measurement methods across studies. At least within services, some consistency needs to be introduced across future studies which will require some collaboration between authorities or at least between researchers.

Those situations most likely to engender violence, and the profiles of the most likely assailants, are relatively clear for the health and social services. However they still need to be explored within education.

EXPLANATIONS OF AGGRESSION AND VIOLENCE

In seeking to explain aggression or violence, it is usual to differentiate between their 'instrumental' and 'emotional' (or angry) forms. Instrumental aggression or violence is primarily a means towards some other end. The policeman shot as bank robbers make their getaway is killed so that they may escape, not because they are angry. Emotional or angry violence or aggression, in contrast, deliberately inflicts injury: doing damage is an end in itself, and any instrumental value it has exists purely at the psychological level. The counter staff who are attacked when benefits are refused are not attacked in order to convince them to award a payment, the attack is driven by anger and the desire to hurt. Most of the attempts to explain aggression or violence have focused upon the emotional variety. The other type of violence is thought to be sufficiently explained because it has an instrumental value.

There are three main types of psychological explanation: the instinct explanation, the social or cultural learning explanation, and the aversive stimulation explanation (of which the frustration–aggression hypothesis represents a special case). They will be described briefly in turn.

THE INSTINCT EXPLANATION

The instinct explanation asserts that humans are genetically preprogrammed to be violent and aggressive. The basic idea is that the urge to be aggressive builds up over time independently of events and must be satisfied – something like the need to eat or sleep. According to this view, we are all aggressive; aggression and violence are inescapable biological imperatives. We differ only in the ways and situations in which we allow our aggression to be released.

Within this framework, the aggressive instinct is assumed to have developed because it has survival value for the species as a whole and, to a lesser extent, for individual members of it. However such an explanation has little usefulness for the practitioner because it has little predictive power. It cannot say when aggression will occur, what form it will take, or what interventions are likely to control it.

THE SOCIAL OR CULTURAL LEARNING EXPLANATION

This focuses upon the assumption that aggression and violence are behaviours like all others and are learned. Two types of learning are said to be involved: instrumental and observational. Instrumental learning is supposed to occur when a behaviour is reinforced through rewards and is therefore more likely to recur in the future. Aggressive acts which are rewarded will be produced more frequently. Reward can take many forms: material (e.g. financial), social (e.g. status), or psychological (e.g. emotional satisfaction). Reward can be achieved through improvements on any of these planes. For example, if a child is successful in getting her own way through using physical force with other children, she will be inclined to use it more frequently. If a pupil can disrupt a class and gain admiration from his peers for doing so, the disruptive activity will increase. Acts which result in the removal of something which is unpleasant are also reinforced and are likely to recur. For instance, a child who prevents another from bullying him by thumping the bully is likely to use violence as a coping strategy in the future.

While some aggressive behaviours can be established through direct reinforcement, many others are believed to be learned through *observation* of others. This is sometimes called social modelling. Bandura and his collaborators (1961) showed that children who watched someone behaving in a violent way towards a large doll would, when subsequently given the opportunity, behave in a similar manner towards the doll. The children were said to be 'modelling' the behaviour of the aggressor. There are many studies with adults which show the importance of modelling (Bandura, 1973). While children may learn *how* to be aggressive by watching others, adults appear to know *when* it is appropriate to be aggressive by the same means.

The learning explanation for aggression and violence can accommodate the existence of cultural and subcultural differences in their amount and the form they take. The argument is that cultures differ in the amount and types of aggression which are available for the child to learn. Anthropological evidence (Gorer, 1968) indicates that some societies emphasise the value of pacifism, and measure achievement in terms of personal gratifications (such as sex, eating or drinking), rather than in terms of dominance or power over others. Similarly, sociological evidence proves that subcultures differ greatly in the ways in which they will allow aggression to be expressed. In some, aggression is expected to be expressed physically, in others, verbally. Subcultures differ in who they expect to be aggressive and when. For instance, there are marked differences between the ways in which they expect men and women to express their aggression.

The fundamental argument of anthropologists and sociologists in this area is that norms which are dominant in a person's society or subculture direct not only the frequency and form of their aggression but also determine its targets, because people learn what behaviour is appropriate. The exercise on pages 46–48 is designed to allow you to examine the forms of violence and aggression you tend to use, and that accord with the norms and expectations of your own subculture.

This type of explanation for aggression has value for the practitioner because it suggests that if you know the norms which control the form, frequency and targets of aggression in the subculture where you work, then you will be better able to predict likely incidents. It does mean that the behaviour of individual clients, patients or pupils would need to be analysed in relation to their social background. Of course this is more possible in some practice contexts than in others: it assumes that you already know something about the individual's background and there are many situations where a practitioner must intervene without having had the opportunity to acquire relevant background information. The social or cultural learning explanation may be particularly valuable for teachers who can learn the subcultural norms about aggression which operate within their particular school. Each school has its own culture and expectations about pupil–teacher relations. Norms on the use of aggression and violence by both teachers and pupils are part of this set of expectations.

THE AVERSIVE STIMULATION EXPLANATION
This focuses on the conditions under which aggression is exhibited. The approach was originally presented in the form of the frustration–

PERSONALLY PREFERRED FORMS OF VIOLENCE OR AGGRESSION

This exercise is designed to help you assess what forms of aggression or violence *you* are likely to exhibit. You may already have a good understanding of your own responses when angry, but this set of questions is designed to illustrate the range of potential responses and indicate how your own pattern relates to it.

For each statement please put a tick in the box which best reflects the frequency with which you respond in that way.

"When angry, I am the sort of person who . . ."

	—A— Usually	—B— Sometimes	—C— Never
1. Becomes cool and deliberately self-controlled	☐	☐	☐
2. Remains calm	☐	☐	☐
3. Becomes verbally vicious	☐	☐	☐
4. Becomes speechless	☐	☐	☐
5. Tries to leave the situation or person generating the anger	☐	☐	☐
6. Wants to hurt someone else	☐	☐	☐
7. Physically attacks the cause of the anger so as to eliminate it	☐	☐	☐
8. Becomes annoyed with myself	☐	☐	☐
9. Feels very guilty	☐	☐	☐
10. Yells or screams	☐	☐	☐
11. Cries	☐	☐	☐
12. Flies into a rage	☐	☐	☐
13. Bottles up the feeling and finds some outlet for it later	☐	☐	☐
14. Fails to tackle the cause of the anger directly	☐	☐	☐

	— A — Usually	— B — Sometimes	— C — Never
15. Thinks about and analyses the angering experience for a long time after	☐	☐	☐
16. Makes threatening gestures at the person who angers me	☐	☐	☐
17. Punishes the person who angers me by withdrawing my affection or respect	☐	☐	☐
18. Loses control of myself	☐	☐	☐
19. Redirects the anger towards inanimate objects (e.g. kicking the furniture)	☐	☐	☐
20. Allows my anger to show in my general demeanour	☐	☐	☐

These questions relate to four dimensions along which aggression may be expressed:

Verbal—Physical

Score	A	B	C
Q 3	3	2	1
Q 4	1	2	3
Q10	3	2	1
Q16	1	2	3
Q17	3	2	1

This dimension reflects the obvious distinction between the expression of anger in words and in actions. It is worth emphasising that the two blend together at points, and that the same person can use both forms of aggression at different times. The important thing is to establish your preferred or habitual mode.

▶ The greater your score, the more you use verbal expressions of aggression and avoid physical aggression.

Direct—Displaced

Score	A	B	C
Q 5	3	2	1
Q 7	1	2	3
Q13	3	2	1
Q14	3	2	1
Q19	3	2	1

The direct–displaced dimension represents the less obvious distinction between aggression which is directed at the reason for your anger and that which is displaced on to other objects. This is the 'kick the cat instead of the boss' phenomenon. Displacement can occur for many reasons: fear or concern for the real object of your anger are the prime causes.

▶ The greater your score, the higher the level of displacement you engage in.

Fury—Calm

	Score		
	A	**B**	**C**
Q 1	3	2	1
Q 2	3	2	1
Q12	1	2	3
Q18	1	2	3
Q20	1	2	3

This reflects the level of self-control you believe you have when angry. People differ in the extent to which they allow anger to be translated into passion. Some, when angry, become calculating and cold.

▶ The higher the score, the greater the level of calmness.

Intrapunitive—Extrapunitive

	Score		
	A	**B**	**C**
Q 6	1	2	3
Q 8	3	2	1
Q 9	3	2	1
Q11	3	2	1
Q15	3	2	1

This dimension refers to the direction of aggression. Intrapunitive responses entail directing aggression inwards, against yourself. Extrapunitive responses entail externalising aggression. Self-blame, self-doubt, shame and guilt can all be forms of intrapunitiveness. Intrapunitiveness has also been linked with various psychosomatic complaints such as asthma and stomach ulcers.

▶ A higher score indicates higher intrapunitiveness.

There are currently no standard scores for the caring professions against which you could compare yourself on these indices. If you want to compare your own responses with those of others in your professional group, you could get some of your colleagues to complete the exercise as well.

aggression hypothesis (Dollard *et al.*, 1939). The hypothesis is simple: all aggression is preceded by frustration of some sort. All frustration does not lead to aggression (it can find expression in other ways), but all aggression has frustration as a precursor. Frustration is defined as the state generated when the individual cannot behave in a manner which will achieve set goals: ongoing goal-directed activity is unexpectedly blocked. There is considerable evidence that frustration can cause aggression, especially if it is intense or if aggression is seen to be likely to result in goal attainment. But frustration does not always result in aggression. For instance, where it does not result in anger or where it is seen to have a justifiable origin, frustration is unlikely to initiate aggression.

Berkowitz (1986) has argued that the relationship between frustration and aggression is actually only a special example of a much more general phenomenon. He suggests that humans are biologically preprogrammed to become aggressive when faced with unpleasant situations. Situations become unpleasant because they generate aversive stimuli. The desire to evade such stimulation increases the individual's level of arousal and, as arousal increases, so does the willingness to behave aggressively.

Frustration is only one sort of unpleasant feeling that people wish to avoid. Physical pain is obviously another. But noise, crowding and heat can act in exactly the same way. Just as frustration can find alternative expression, so other unpleasant experiences do not necessarily give rise to aggression. Whether they do, Berkowitz says, depends on the precise nature of the situation in which they occur, the past history of the person involved, and his or her genetic predispositions. Painful experiences can result in avoidance or flight instead of aggression. There is considerable empirical evidence to suggest that painful experiences are most likely to result in aggression if the individual has a history of aggressive responses (particularly if these have been found to be effective in gaining rewards), if aggression is likely to eradicate them, or if there are cues for violence prevalent in the situation. Where cues are present which are culturally associated with violence, for instance a weapon of some sort or people who symbolise violence (boxers for instance), then aggression is a more frequent response to unpleasant stimulation.

If much aggression and violence can be considered simply as a predictable response to unpleasant experiences, the frequency with which professionals experience hostility becomes hardly surprising. Most of them are, after all, called in precisely at those times when their clients or patients are dealing with events which are unpleasant and distressing. The nurse in the emergency department of a hospital will, throughout a night's duty, be expected to offer practical and emotional support to people who have been frightened and are in pain and may be suffering severe anxiety. Sometimes practitioners themselves represent the unpleasant experience – for instance, when a social worker tells a family that one of its members should be compulsorily detained in a psychiatric hospital under the Mental Health Act, or when a health visitor suggests that a child is deaf, or when a doctor admits that a condition is inoperable. In each case, it is the practitioner who generates the unpleasant information.

INTERPRETING SITUATIONS

Our responses to aversive stimuli are greatly influenced by the way we perceive the situation. People will tolerate considerable pain and discomfort or frustration without becoming aggressive if they interpret the situation to have arisen unintentionally or accidentally. It is, of course, important to add that there are situations in which some people will be aggressive, even though they know that the discomfort was not deliberately intended. The inhibitors which would normally curtail aggression in response to unintended hurt can break down. The ability to inhibit the expression of aggression is markedly affected by drinking and certain drugs. For instance, there is a body of evidence to support the popular idea that alcohol in moderate quantities will increase aggressive behaviour, though it should be said that there are big differences between individuals in how disinhibited they are by alcohol. Individual inhibitions against violence are also often ignored if the person is enmeshed in group activity.

The particular value of the aversive stimulation explanation of aggression and violence lies in its power to bridge the gap between the instinct and social learning theories. It acknowledges the biological and physiological foundations for aggression but also emphasises the way socially determined ways of interpreting events will channel the potential for aggression and its expression. It shows that behaviour is not predetermined by instincts nor based solely on learning or modelling. Instead, it recognises that there is a complex symbolic world through which people navigate a course and in which aggression has an important role. The meaning of and reasons for an aversive event will in part determine whether it elicits violence or aggression. But equally the potentially aggressive response will also carry with it many different implications, some of which will determine whether it is actually carried through in a particular situation, or whether an alternative non-violent response occurs. The individual's understanding of the events has a big part to play in directing aggression. The perception of the cause for the aversive experience, the mitigating circumstances which may apply, the impact of aggression on what others may think of one, the likely benefits of aggression; all these have a part to play in predicting aggression. In acknowledging these factors, the aversive

stimulation explanation acknowledges the importance of the way people gather, store and handle information in violence and aggression. It
is also implicitly arguing for the *malleability* of aggression, since these
habits of thought can be influenced and changed.

Given the paradoxical role of most of the caring professions (as
discussed on p. 14) it may be impossible to remove the aversive stimuli
which encourage aggression. It is therefore more practical for practitioners to modify the way in which these stimuli are *interpreted* or the
ways in which the aggression is expressed.

To return to an earlier example: the junior nurse in the emergency
ward at night may not be able to remove patients' fear, pain or much of
their anxiety, but she might be able to ensure that any delay in
treatment is explained so that it does not become another cause for
distress and she is not seen as deliberately hostile.

For the practitioner, the aversive stimuli explanation of aggression
and violence also has some value because it highlights the types of
circumstance in which they are likely to occur. This type of explanation
does make it possible to anticipate the broad range of situations in
which violence is likely and the sorts of factor which will increase its
likelihood.

VIOLENCE IN A GROUP CONTEXT

So far in discussing the forms of aggression and violence it has been
implicit that these are the acts of individuals. In fact, it is necessary to
distinguish *individuals* who are aggressive or violent and *groups* or
organisations which are aggressive or violent. Violence can emanate
from all sorts of group: from those as informal and unstructured as
crowds to those as complex and hierarchical as large corporations. It
can range from the police-stoning street riot to the corporate vandalism
involved in making entire communities redundant. Similarly, groups
can engage in aggression: street gangs can induce terror with threats,
business consortia can foster desperation with rumours of closure.

Obviously, even in groups or organisations it is individuals who
produce the violence or aggression, but the underlying pattern of
responsibility is different. The decision to be aggressive or violent does
not rest entirely with the individual. Responsibility is diffused across
group or organisation members. Such diffusion of responsibility has
long been assumed to explain partially why people are more violent,
irrational and full of hostile emotions when part of a group than when
acting as isolated individuals. They feel anonymous in the group and
therefore feel that they can get away metaphorically, and sometimes

literally, with murder because they are an unidentifiable part of the mass. This process of losing the self in the group is known as *de-individuation*.

There is a contradictory explanation for why people behave more violently when part of a crowd. This suggests that extremes of behaviour occur in groups not because people lose their sense of self or forget the norms which usually control their behaviour, but rather because *new norms* emerge within a crowd in a specific situation. So, for instance, in a street riot, the crowd can generate the idea that it is necessary to protect itself from the police. Stoning the police becomes the norm for the situation, even though it abrogates commonly held pre-existing norms.

More importantly, in high-stress situations even well-organised groups tend to become concerned with maintaining group cohesion and survival to the exclusion of rationality. Under such circumstances, they become subject to what Janis (1976) called 'groupthink'. This is a state characterised by the belief that whatever the group decides is right and morally acceptable, and that any challenge to the group's decision from within constitutes treachery. Violence towards anyone not allied to the group is then regarded as morally appropriate.

It is evident that forms of violence and aggression involving groups or organisations must be treated differently from those concerning isolated individuals. It is probably true that the caring professions mainly face violence from individuals. But it is also true that family groups can be a considerable threat for anyone working in the community. When youths come together in gangs they can also generate incidents in educational and residential settings.

It has become clear in considering various explanations of violence and aggression that neither can be explained in terms of individual psychological processes. Violence and aggression must be seen as embedded in the interactions between two or more people, in the particular circumstances in which they find themselves and against the backdrop of the cultural norms which guide their actions.

ANTICIPATING WHAT KIND OF VIOLENCE

Up till now the circumstances in which people find themselves – the 'when' and the 'where' of aggression – have been examined in order to understand aggression more fully, with the aim of predicting it successfully. But an understanding of what *kind* of violence is also needed in order to avoid or control it. In calculating the probability of particular kinds of violence, it is most helpful to use what is known about subcultural and situational norms concerning violence in collaboration with whatever is known about the past behaviour of the potential aggressor. In this sense, it is necessary to marry the social or cultural learning explanations and the aversive stimuli explanation of aggression in order to arrive at any usable basis for an estimate of risk.

GENERAL AND SPECIFIC CLUES

General theories of aggression clearly have to be distinguished from the sorts of specific explanation for particular violent incidents which are commonly produced by the participants or by observers. Accounts by observers are likely to emphasise the assailant's personality and the unique combination of traits which characterise him or her. Accounts by the assailant are likely to focus upon the context and its unique combination of circumstances. In contrast, the theories are based on generic principles which provide insights about the likelihood of violence at a very general level. At that general level they suggest a list of clues as to the amount of risk involved.

Generally risk is greater if:

- The person is a member of a group or subculture where physical violence is the norm. A violent person will therefore experience no loss of face (and may, in fact, gain social approval).

- The person has a history of violence – violence is then assumed to be a preferred strategy for dealing with problems.

- The person is aroused by something unpleasant (especially if this is interpreted as a deliberate attempt to hurt and as directed specifically at him or her).

- The person is disinhibited (through drugs, alcohol, deindividuation, physical illnesses such as brain damage, etc.).

- The person expects the violence to be rewarded (either materially or through social approval).

- The person believes no other action is possible. This may be associated with a belief that the person is not in control of his or her own actions (this owes something to the instinct theories of aggression).

There are, however, other clues which can be used when calculating risk in a specific situation which are not dependent on general explanations of aggression. These stem from empirical research on the expression of aggression.

Risk is greater in a specific situation if:

- The person has been threatening violence – threats can have an end in themselves if they are designed to control or scare, but they can also represent a statement of intention. Intentions are the best known predictors of action – much better than attitudes, beliefs or values.

- There are cues to violence in the situation (e.g. the presence of knives, choppers or other weapons, or if someone else is already acting violently).

- The person shows physiological signs of high arousal. Unfortunately these are by no means simple to detect: some people display a flushed skin reflecting raised blood pressure, perspiration, increased muscle tension, heightened respiration rate and pulse, and even nausea, but for others arousal causes loss of colour and great stillness. The real clue seems to be any *shift* from the individual's typical state.

- The person is verbally abusive – verbal abuse is a frequent but not inevitable precursor to violence. Also, tone, pitch and speed of talk can change. Again it is variation from the person's typical pattern which should be treated with caution.

- There is peer group pressure being exerted upon the person to be violent.

- The person is showing non-verbal signs of imminent violence: invasion of personal space (that invisible bubble which surrounds each of us and which we regard as our inalienable mobile territory); maintenance of eye contact for prolonged periods so that it becomes uncomfortable; rapid unpredictable arm movements, especially pointing, clenching and unclenching teeth or fists, etc. Again, non-verbal signs can only be interpreted against the backdrop of the person's typical behaviour. Deviations from the norm provide useful cues.

Taken together, these clues can provide a useful basis for calculations of risk. But anyone using the list as a guide must understand that there are no cast-iron rules for predicting specific occurrences of violence. There is no set equation which summarises what constellation of clues will always precede violence. Each violent incident is unique. In some, none of these clues will be present. But in the majority, at least some clues will be there to provide a warning for those who can see them.

Chapter Four

Avoidance, Escape and Control

Consider the following scenarios and decide what you would do in each case.

YOU HAVE JUST JOINED THE TEACHING STAFF AT A SCHOOL. *One of the male pupils, aged 14, is disruptive in the first class you take him for. He ignores your instructions to behave and is being egged on by a small band of other pupils. When you order him to be silent, he threatens to 'see to you later'.*

YOU ARE A SOCIAL WORKER *whose long-term schizophrenic client has attacked his elderly parents again, and you are asked to make an assessment with a psychiatrist with a view to taking him compulsorily into a psychiatric hospital. Before you get to his house, he disappears but is reported to have gone down the road to a local community centre.*

In deciding what to do, what factors would you consider? What additional information would you require before estimating the risk involved? What assumptions would you make about the person you are dealing with in each case? Having calculated the risk, what would you seek to do to ensure your own safety? How would your strategies for ensuring your safety differ in the two scenarios? It would be useful to compare the answers you give now to these questions with the answers you give after reading the chapter.

UNDERLYING OBJECTIVES

In making suggestions about the ways in which violence can be handled, one of the clear objectives is to increase practitioner safety. However, any recommendations are also influenced by three other underlying objectives. Firstly, the strategies for coping with violence must be professionally acceptable: they must not undermine the fundamental values of the caring professions. Secondly, the strategies should not alienate clients, patients or pupils. Alienating the violent themselves may not be seen to be a problem but alienating others who are not dangerous by imposing general rules for practioner protection may well become a problem. Finally, the strategies must equate with the image of themselves which the practitioners' employers wish to maintain. This will in turn be affected by the political and economic environment in which employers must operate.

Both the explicit and implicit objectives will shape the actual practical viability of any recommendation. In the end, the package of avoidance, protection and control strategies adopted will depend upon the preoccupations of individual practitioners and the priorities of the organisations within which they work. Most of the strategies entail simultaneous changes in the practice of individuals and in the procedures of the system.

STRATEGIES OF AVOIDANCE

Practitioners should avoid situations where violence is likely. This is obviously not always feasible, but where avoidance is possible it should be recognised as an *honourable* option. Avoidance can only be achieved if the practitioner has the information which will provide the basis for accurate prediction of the behaviour of the client, pupil or patient.

PREDICTING VIOLENCE

VIOLENCE TOWARDS OTHERS

The notion of using predictors of behaviour is commonly accepted in the caring professions. One of the most widely used, yet controversial, set of predictors concerns child abuse. Researchers (Gardner and Gray, 1982) have shown that those who abuse their children tend to have an identifiable profile. They are likely to be isolated from their family and friends, they are involved in marital conflict, they wanted a child of the opposite sex, they live in deprived social and economic conditions, they have unrealistic expectations of the child's behaviour and perceive the child to be deliberately wilful or naughty, and they have an idealistic image of what parenthood should be like. They also tend to have no way of handling conflict other than by becoming violent. It is also possible to profile the child who is abused, since prematurity, mental retardation, physical handicap, and perinatal complications are overrepresented in the abused population.

The important point to remember about predictors is that they result in *overinclusion* of suspects. Not all who have this profile will be abusers. The predictors simply allow attention to be focused upon people most at risk of abusing. These individuals can then be more intensively monitored.

Predictors can also be used to identify children who are likely to be repeatedly involved in serious crimes later in life. Farrington (1987) argues that there is continuity between childhood trouble and adult criminal behaviour. Frequent serious offenders tend to have had: harsh or erratic parental discipline, parents whose attitude was cruel, passive or neglectful, poor parental supervision during childhood and parents who were themselves in conflict before the child was eight years old. Again, not everyone with this profile becomes a criminal. The predictors act to target a broad group of people and will include some who would never become criminals. People with this type of background who remain law-abiding are characterised by higher intelligence, greater shyness, anxiety and apathy, and the tendency to be withdrawn or obsessional. They also tend to come from families with fewer children and where the parents did not separate or become involved in serious conflicts. Farrington suggests that any intervention designed to prevent the shift into criminality (such as training for parents or the provision of special tutoring in school) should be over-inclusive in its catchment. This approach means that the predictors can still be used even though they are somewhat insensitive to individual variations.

From the point of view of the practitioner seeking to avoid violent confrontation, both the predictors of child abuse and the predictors of frequent serious offending are tangentially useful because, for a reasonably large number of practitioners (for example, social workers, probation officers, police officers), people with this background will comprise major client groups. It is therefore useful supplementary information in predicting behaviour.

VIOLENCE TOWARDS PRACTITIONERS
Predictors of violence towards the practitioner can be developed from the body of research summarised in Chapter 3. These are listed in their simplest form in The Dangerousness Checklist. The Checklist can be

— THE DANGEROUSNESS CHECKLIST —

When assessing the extent of the risk of violence in a situation you are about to enter you should consider the following questions. The more often you answer 'yes', the greater the risk of violence.

▶ Is the person I am dealing with facing high levels of stress?
▶ Is the person likely to be drunk or on drugs?
▶ Does the person have a history of violence?
▶ Does the person have a history of criminal convictions?
▶ Does the person have a history of psychiatric illness?
▶ Does the person suffer from a medical condition which may result in loss of self-control?
▶ Has the person verbally abused me in the past?
▶ Has the person threatened me with violence in the past?
▶ Has the person attacked me in the past?
▶ Does the person perceive me as a threat to his/her children?
▶ Does the person think of me as a threat to his/her liberty?
▶ Does the person have unrealistic expectations of what I can do for him/her?
▶ Does the person perceive me as wilfully unhelpful?
▶ Have I felt anxious for my safety with this person before?
▶ Are other people present who will reward the person for violence?

Facing the client or patient, other cues should be examined. Again, the more times you answer 'yes' in a situation, the greater the danger:

▶ Is the person showing signs of atypical excitement or passivity?
▶ Are there weapons or similar cues to violence in the room?
▶ Is the person showing signs of atypical high arousal?
▶ Is there a breakdown in the normal pattern of nonverbal communication?
▶ Is the person showing signs of rapid mood swings?
▶ Is the person oversensitive to suggestions or criticisms?

The implications of the risk are greater if you answer 'yes' to several of the following questions:

▶ Am I alone and without back-up?
▶ Are colleagues unaware of my whereabouts?
▶ Am I without any means of raising the alarm if attacked?
▶ Am I likely to be trapped without an escape route if the person becomes violent?
▶ Am I unaware of how I react in violent situations?
▶ Am I unaware of the assault cycle?
▶ Am I unaware of the cultural norms which are likely to control this person's exhibition of violence?
▶ Have I ever considered what I would do if attacked?

used as a barometer of the risk of violence during any professional contacts. You should mentally run through the list regularly, prior to contacts. In order to answer some of the questions it is necessary to have considerable information on the other person involved. This will only be available to individual practitioners if good communication systems (especially across agencies, e.g. police to social services and from them to the education system) are set up, and if better records of contacts and incidents are kept.

If the risk is calculated to be great, two major avoidance strategies should be considered:

1. Do not proceed to make contact: report your estimate of the risk to your line manager, supervisor or senior colleague and come to a joint decision about the appropriate course of action.

2. Make a preliminary contact: this can entail indirect contact (e.g. telephoning to check details which may influence your estimate of risk), or it may entail writing to rearrange the venue or time for the contact so that back-up is available if trouble occurs (back-up could involve having a colleague present).

The first option should be regarded as your best response. Of course, it will only be useful if practitioners operating in senior or middle management roles accept that it is part of their job to develop corporate plans for dealing with a person who is considered risky. While the response to each high-risk contact will need to be individually tailored, it is also possible to develop general guidelines over time which suit your own particular department, team or institution. One particularly attractive proposition is the use of specialists trained to take over high-risk contacts.

The second option may not be feasible in some contexts; for example, in schools or hospitals. It is mainly viable for practitioners outside institutional contexts. It should also be embedded in generally acknowledged procedures where possible.

Even where estimates of risk indicate that avoidance would be sensible, it is not always possible. It may not be possible to do the job without making high-risk contacts on a regular basis. For instance, it would be farcical to suggest that a nurse doing night duty in an accident ward could simply ignore the needs of a belligerent but injured drunk even though she knows that all of the predictors indicate high risk. The fact that she will anticipate trouble, even though she cannot avoid it, is one precursor to self-protection. There are others which can be used. Sections B and C in The Dangerousness Checklist are included as reminders of the factors which need to be considered once the contact has been made. Again, the more times you answer 'yes', the greater the risk.

CALCULATING RISKS

The problem with relying upon estimates of risk is that people are notoriously bad at calculating probabilities accurately. They find it difficult to say for instance whether an event has a 1 in 10 or 1 in 100 chance of happening. Even when they are completely aware of all the necessary information, they tend to produce biased estimates. They are influenced by their own prejudices, by recent experiences, by their own emotional involvement and so on. Estimates of risk are, therefore, rarely accurate. Becoming aware of the processes which influence your own probability calculations can be the first step towards a more accurate perception of the risks in any particular situation.

There are three major biases which have been identified (Kahneman *et al.*, 1982): availability, anchoring and adjustments, and representativeness.

AVAILABILITY
People make poor estimates of the *frequency* of events. They tend to be overly influenced by how easily specific instances can be brought to mind. For instance, they may assess the risk of heart attack among middle-aged men on the basis of the number of their acquaintances who have suffered one, because this is prominent in their memory. Obviously, this leads to biased estimates of risk unless the number of instances recalled is proportional to the actual incidence rate. In fact, most estimates of risk are biased in this way because we believe that easily remembered examples occur more frequently. So, someone who had a colleague who was physically assaulted might be influenced by this recollection and would assume that the frequency of assault was greater than it actually is. In such a case, estimates of risk are affected by *familiarity* with an example.

We are also influenced by the *importance* and *relevance* of the example. Both of these features will affect the ease with which it is initially stored in our memory and subsequently retrieved. It is notable that, once alerted to a risk through personal experience, people can become selectively attentive to information relevant to it. For instance, the death of a good friend from a heart attack will result in the person paying more attention to reports of other such deaths. If the friend also smoked heavily, the link between smoking and coronary disease would be emphasised. Once established, this link would encourage the person to look for evidence of heavy smoking in all coronary cases. This can mean that a sort of snowball effect occurs with more and more examples which support the initial conclusion being stored away and used as the foundation for future calculations of risk. Of course, this has the effect of increasing the level of perceived risk.

The availability of examples is also affected by the *information retrieval strategy* adopted in the first place. Our memories can be searched in many ways in order to generate relevant information for the calculation of probabilities. In order to estimate the probability of violence, the search could be organised around memories of personal incidents, press coverage of serious attacks, conversations in which assaults were described and so on. The method used for eliciting and organising our memories will bias the type and amount of information collected. For instance, memories relating to ourselves are more easily retrieved, especially if they provide a positive picture of us. Probabilities based on such memories will be likely therefore to underestimate potential hazards. Basically, some retrieval strategies are more comprehensive and thus more effective than others in generating accurate estimates of probability.

Imagination also plays an important role in the evaluation of probabilities. The risk involved in meeting someone else is evaluated by imagining eventualities with which it would be impossible to cope. If difficulties can be vividly imagined, the risk is likely to be judged higher. In contrast, when our imagination fails, risks are perceived to be less. This is all irrespective of the actual statistical probability of danger.

People are particularly influenced in estimates of risk by *preconceptions* about associations between events or things. If two things are associated with each other in popular belief (for example red hair and bad temper), when people are presented with one of the pair, they tend to assume the other is present regardless of whether they have any justification for that assumption. For instance, if GPs in a particular area believe that one local council estate is dangerous to visit at night, when they hear that a GP has been mugged at night in the area they are very likely to assume that it was in the same council estate. They are then likely to remember the incident as occurring in the estate, even if their assumption is later proved wrong. More importantly, this erroneous information will then feed into any further calculations of the risks of going to that estate.

ANCHORING AND ADJUSTMENT

In calculating risk, people tend to start from an initial estimate and then adjust this to produce a final estimate. They might assume that they have a 1 in 50 chance of being attacked in a year. This estimate will be modified to take account of additional information which supports it in particular situations. However, there is considerable evidence to show that people do not shift enough from their original estimate when faced with evidence which contradicts their preconceptions.

Bias due to anchoring is exemplified in another way. People tend to generalise too easily from one success to others. So, for instance, a practitioner who successfully handled one potentially violent situation is likely to infer that the risks in other violent situations are lower than they actually are. It seems that people are more likely to assume that the same pattern of events will recur than they are to assume that there will be a break with what happened before.

REPRESENTATIVENESS

Many probability estimates require the person to say whether an event or an individual belongs to a particular category. If they do, assumptions can be made about the probability that they will possess certain characteristics. Typically, people fail to make use of the appropriate information when making such categorisations. They ignore the overall number of people or events in the category. If the description of the event or person fits the stereotype held of the category, the probability of them being members of it is considered high, even if it is known that the membership of the category is very small. For instance, given a description of Joe as impatient, irritable, verbally abusive and a heavy drinker, a social worker when asked to say whether or not he is violent is likely to say that there is a high probability that he is. Furthermore, such an estimate is likely to be believed forcefully. The closer the match between the individual's description and the stereotype, the greater the confidence with which the prediction is made.

In drawing conclusions about the probability of an event people are also willing to base massive generalisations on very small samples. So, for instance, they are willing to make generalisations from two or three examples of violent incidents, to the probability of such events generally. They tend to ignore information about the representativeness of the events. Their conclusions also seem to fail to take account of chance variability, that is, they are willing to generalise from one event without recognising that it may be a completely atypical random occurrence.

Each of these three major biases in estimates of probability will influence the perception of risk. Calculations of their impact cannot be made with any certainty because in reality they push and pull in different directions: some promote overestimation, some underestimation of risk. Since accurate risk calculation is vital when trying to cope with violence in the caring professions, individual practitioners need to make themselves aware of the sorts of bias which characterise their estimates. For instance:

? What stereotypes of violent people do you hold?

? What sorts of people do you expect to be violent?

? How surprised would you be if someone without these characteristics were violent with you?

? What preconceptions do you have about the level of risk you personally are at?

? Is it once a year, once a month, once a week that you are at risk?

? How often do you revise your estimates of risk?

? How frequently do you face a potentially violent situation?

? Is your estimate of your own risk level being influenced by recent examples of dangerous situations you have been in or heard about?

The object in answering these questions is simply to get to grips with the personal background considerations which will influence your estimates of risk.

There is one further form of bias worth mentioning here. Familiarity with a situation appears to breed confidence and to reduce perceived risks. People familiar with a situation develop a sense of *subjective immunity* from its dangers. Even when they recognise the risks at some general, in principle, level for other people, they still regard themselves to be invulnerable. This pattern of risk perception has been found in many contexts. Farmers living on flood plains, even though they know other farms have been flooded and destroyed, still stay, arguing that it will never happen to them. Smokers, knowing the risk of cancer and cardiovascular disease, continue to argue that *they* won't suffer. Those living next to nuclear power plants rate the risks of radiation as lower than do those living further afield. Similarly, members of the caring professions who regularly face dangerous situations are likely to minimise the risks involved. This can, of course, be a way of handling fear by denying danger. But it is counterproductive, since it may hinder the anticipation and avoidance of violence. The point to emphasise is that people's perception of personal risk may not equate with their perception of the risk faced by others. The sense of subjective immunity is something which most practitioners must curb in the interests of accurately understanding the nature of their relationship with client, patient or pupil.

PROTECTION AND ESCAPE

Assuming that practitioners will always need to put themselves at risk in order to do their work, the next task is to provide them with protection. Practitioners can do some things to protect themselves but most strategies also require organisational changes.

ORGANISATIONAL STRATEGIES

The most popular recommendations concerning protection, (including those from Strathclyde Regional Council, 1986; Brown *et al.*, 1986; Owens and Ashcroft, 1985 and Crane, 1986) are listed below. Most echo those suggested by the Health Services Commission which were summarised in Chapter 3.

1. Make alarm systems available – either personal alarms or room alarms.

2. Use video systems to monitor isolated areas, or communal areas where staff work alone, so that any assault will be visible to other staff.

3. Design reception areas so that there is no easy access to staff.

4. Improve staffing levels so as to provide the personnel necessary for back-up if trouble occurs.

5. Make known the location and movements of staff so that any deviation from the planned timetable can be used as a signal that trouble may have occurred and assistance can be quickly organised. (Portable telephones for field staff make this system possible.)

6. Have routine liaison with the police force so that they can be called in quickly.

These recommendations have been criticised by some for reflecting a 'fortress mentality' which is antithetical to the beliefs of many carers. They are also costly to execute. Relatively few employers have yet put them into practice and there is little sign that more will in the near future. This means that the practitioner must take responsibility *individually* for protection in high-risk situations.

SELF-HELP STRATEGIES

Unfortunately few practitioners know how they should behave when facing a violent client, pupil or patient. You may wish to consider what action you think would be best if you were faced with a youth holding a broken bottle who is hesitating just before striking you; or what action you think would be best if you encountered a frantic seminaked woman at the head of the stairs carrying her recently dead baby. One study of social workers showed that most people, when asked how they would respond to threatened violence, eventually said they would try to reason with the assailant or to move away slowly. The truth is, however, that those with experience of assault knew that in the real situation they had most frequently frozen and failed to respond. They were too shocked and surprised by the turn of events.

If you have gone through The Dangerousness Checklist regularly (see page 59) and calculated the risk of violence before contact is made, violence will not take you by surprise when it occurs. Mental rehearsal of what alternative strategies are open to you in the face of violence is valuable. Going calmly through your available options many times beforehand will make it easier for you to respond swiftly in the crisis situation. This will prevent personal injury and any escalation of the incident.

Useful strategies frequently recommended include:

1. Give the impression of being calm, self-controlled and confident without being dismissive or overbearing.

2. Keep talking, using as normal a tone of voice as possible. Changes of tone have sometimes been used to attract the attention of an assailant who is manic. Mood-matching is sometimes useful: the assailant who shouts is shouted at; calm intensity is greeted with equal intensity.

3. Try diversionary tactics (e.g. offer to make tea, claim to be worried about something outside, say you are hungry, make jokes).

4. If the attack is designed to establish the assailant's dominance (as

may happen in sexual assaults) feign submission, using talk to redirect attention.

5. As soon as the risk of attack is evident check on the availability of escape routes or exits and work your way towards them. Try to put some large object between yourself and the assailant or manoeuvre so that you are not trapped in a corner.

6. Do not approach an armed assailant; maintain your distance.

7. An armed assailant should be explicitly asked to put the weapon down. You should try to take the initiative where possible in telling the assailant what you want him or her to do. Slow repetition of instructions may be necessary.

8. Remove potential weapons where possible.

9. Try to disperse any onlookers who may be acting to incite the assailant. It is worth noting that it may be naive to expect any assistance from onlookers, even when they have no affiliation with the assailant. Bystander apathy is a well-established phenomenon: when people are in a crowd or group, especially in contexts where they are unknown or unsure of their responsibility, they will not step in to provide help to someone else.

10. Break such bystander apathy by making a highly specific request for assistance from a particular person in the crowd. The trick is to identify someone and give them precise instructions about what they should do.

11. Use nonverbal communication to calm the situation. This is not so easy to do in practice as it may sound. Commentators give different advice. Some claim that you should maintain eye contact (looking straight into the eyes) with the assailant; others say this can be interpreted as aggressive and should be avoided. Some claim sudden movements will arouse retaliation; others that stillness will incite an onslaught. In reality, it is impossible to make generalisations about the role of nonverbal communication in such contexts. Much will depend upon the pattern of previous interactions with the assailant and the reason for the attack. The vital thing is that you should be aware that this form of communication may be operating during the attack. Where a violent incident lasts longer than a few minutes (and some have been known to last for hours) it may be possible to judge which patterns of nonverbal responses will be most effective.

ANXIETY MANAGEMENT

All of the strategies recommended above rely upon you remaining reasonably calm. They would be impossible for anyone who was unable to manage their own anxiety. Anxiety management techniques are based upon knowing how you personally respond to stress. You need to understand what physiological and psychological consequences stress produces (these were described in Chapter 2) and also be familiar with a range of tactics for reducing their effects. Training for handling aggression should include methods of anxiety management.

One of the key factors in reducing the anxiety response in violent situations is the mental rehearsal of coping strategies prior to the event. Just considering the risk and the possibilities introduces a mental hardiness which is invaluable. This is really a variant of the more traditional methods of anxiety management which involved 'desensitising' unpleasant objects or events by associating them with deep relaxation.

Two other techniques are commonly used in anxiety management. The first involves learning to relax muscular tension at will. If you practise relaxing your muscles in a stress-free situation, you will become able to do the same in response to threat. The second technique entails 'positive guided imagery', which basically means thinking about nicer things and better times in the face of adversity. This technique may not be practicable in the face of violence but it may be something to be considered after the event to restore well-being.

As long as anxiety can be held at bay when facing violence, it is possible in any extended incident to use standard counselling skills to top up the recommended approaches described above. This means that basic training for many professionals needs to be extended to encompass counselling skills. Such skills would include knowing how to use assertiveness appropriately, that is, knowing how to acknowledge other people's feelings and rights and still resist them.

Survivors of violent assaults have attested to the usefulness of the strategies recommended above. For instance, one social worker who was tied up by a woman and threatened with a crossbow reported later that there were four aspects of his behaviour during the assault which in retrospect he felt to have been correct:

1. He had been assertive and acknowledged the demand she was making which triggered the incident (she wanted him to write to the housing office to seek a transfer for her) but refused to comply with the demand.

2. He had challenged her and called her bluff when she first produced the crossbow, calmly telling her to put it away.

3. He had used diversionary tactics (claiming he was a vegetarian and would be difficult to hold hostage because she would not be able to feed him; trying to get her to pass on a message to get his dog fed).

4. He had controlled his anxiety by holding on to the thought that the incident would eventually end safely.

Another example comes from a health visitor who went to visit a woman suffering from depression whose child had eczema. She arrived at the house to find the husband wielding an axe. The health visitor had no information on the family since they were new to the area and had been a self-referral. Faced with the axe, she tried diversionary tactics. Noticing that there were voodoo artefacts in the room, she began to talk about the man's voodoo practices. She was ultimately allowed to leave once the conversation finished.

CONTROLLING A VIOLENT SITUATION

PHYSICAL RESTRAINT
One way to control violence is to use force. The legal position is that the carer should use *minimum reasonable force* (that is, enough to stop the aggressor and protect yourself but no more). The general assumption is that the force should focus on restraint being used to overpower the attacker rather than to injure. There is no place for the macho syndrome which calls for force to be met with force. Common guidelines for physical restraint recommend that the person is held near a major joint to avoid dislocation, and not near the throat, neck, chest, abdomen or fingers. Physical restraint is really only feasible if you know you can call upon assistance. It is best to avoid involving other clients in the restraint of an assailant. Restraint needs to be followed up with removal of the assailant from the scene of the violence and isolation is typically used. If you can anticipate that restraint will be necessary it may be as well to involve the police at the earliest opportunity. Police can enter dwellings to prevent a breach of the peace, so anyone who reckons that the risks are great can arrange to have a constable by their side.

THE ASSAULT CYCLE

Physical restraint may control the immediate manifestations of violence but it would be an error to assume that the incident ceases once restraint is achieved. Kaplan and Wheeler (1983) argue that an assault may be visualised as a cycle of phases: the triggering phase, the escalation phase, the crisis phase, the recovery phase, and the post-crisis depression phase. This sequence is in part determined by the sympathetic nervous system's response to the sources of stress in the assault situation: the adrenalin which is secreted in response to threat takes time to be manifested in bodily symptoms (rapid heartbeat, cold sweat, dry throat, shaking, upset stomach) and takes longer to subside. The assault cycle is no respecter of persons and both the assailant and the victim will experience it. The effects on the victim are considered in the next chapter, but the important point here is that the crisis phase for the assailant may last for up to 90 minutes after the initial incident. During that time the person is particularly sensitive to any incitement to violence. This means that there is a strong possibility of renewal of the assault after physical restraint is removed. It is worth anticipating this.

In institutional contexts controlling the assault cycle can be tackled in a different way. Where the violence is minor, a convention of imposing 'time outs' can be implemented. The person who is showing signs of aggression is asked to go to a room set aside for the purpose, stays there alone for a short time and then returns. Time outs are designed to allow arousal levels to drop naturally and thus to de-escalate the situation. They are sometimes supplemented by the use of more explicit programmes designed to discourage the behaviour. These rely upon negatively reinforcing (that is, punishing or failing to reward, for instance by withdrawing privileges) unwanted aggression. As a means of control of violence in practice, these methods are only viable in contexts where the practitioner has fairly long-term control over the things which the person finds rewarding or punishing. They can also only be pursued after a full analysis of the *functions* which the violent behaviour serves. It is only by understanding what the violence is aimed at achieving that it is possible to shape a schedule of rewards or punishments which can eradicate it. Such analyses are also rather difficult in the short term or outside of an institutional setting. If behaviour modification techniques are used it is worth noting that the reinforcement regime should be routinised so that there is no opportunity for intermittent (and consequently very powerful) reinforcement of violent acts. It is also worth bearing in mind that after the violent acts are curtailed by behaviour modification, there may be a 'final fling' of violent activity. This should be anticipated and its effects minimised, possibly through containment.

All these forms of control of violence are centred upon intervention with a particular individual. Many of the caring professions are now arguing that there should be an attempt at *social* control of violence. This would entail campaigns to change attitudes about what is acceptable behaviour in relation to the caring professions. The idea is that the mass media could lead people to view carers and their professional roles in a different light. The problem with such a response to the incidence of violence is that even if people's attitudes could be changed, there is no assurance that their behaviour would follow suit.

IN CONCLUSION . . .

The refrain echoing through everything above is that individual practitioners and the organisations for which they work must act in tandem to cope with violence. The central argument in this chapter has been that practitioners should use all available predictors of violence to estimate the risks they face, even though the predictors will indicate that some contacts are dangerous which prove to be perfectly safe. It is better to be sensitised to contacts which prove safe, than to fail to pinpoint ones which prove hazardous. A procedure should be established by the agency or institution for handling high-risk contacts. This should include the provision of technological gadgetry for maintaining contact and any other material changes in office equipment or design which will maximise staff safety. Before going into a risky situation, strategies for handling violence should be rehearsed. Dogmatic statements about what should be done in any specific situation are pointless. The individual involved must be ready to analyse all available information and choose his or her strategies, a choice which will be heavily influenced by self-knowledge. Such tactical decisions can only be made properly if the individual can remain calm. Familiarity with anxiety management techniques could be productively harnessed in such situations. Escape should be the prime objective in most cases. Attempts to control violence should be limited to restraint or the use of programmes designed to discourage the behaviour.

Chapter Five

Life After Attack

Consider what you would do and feel in the following situations:

YOU ARE A SISTER IN A LARGE TEACHING HOSPITAL. *While you are off-duty one night, a nurse with whom you have often worked is seriously assaulted. The attack includes sexual assault. You hear about it the next day and see the victim immediately since she has been admitted to your ward.*

YOU ARE A HEALTH VISITOR. *Upon a visit to the house of a young woman with a new baby, you are accused of interference by the woman's lover because you point out that the child is not gaining weight at the expected rate. You explain that you are trying to help. He becomes angry and starts shouting. The young woman intervenes to quiet him but he pushes her aside and starts to slap her. You then try to get between them and grab his arm, pushing him backwards. He switches his attack to you. You are bruised and your lip is cut before his attack subsides and you are able to escape.*

Compare what you think you would do, say and feel now with how you would tackle these situations after reading the chapter. You could then consider how you would handle the two victims of assault if you were their line manager or senior colleague. For the first scenario, you should also consider the role of a manager in helping the nursing sister, who has not been attacked personally but who is also affected by the attack.

TYPICAL REACTIONS AFTER ASSAULT

It is useful to know how people commonly react to assault, especially if you are suffering from the effects yourself. It is sometimes reassuring to know that the way in which you are reacting is not unique or in some way wrong or unexpected. Unfortunately, there is actually very little evidence about the effects of assault upon practitioners. There is anecdotal information but any generalisations must be based upon what we know of the effects of violent assault upon victims generally. The response seems to have a number of stages (Hopkins, 1987), two of which comprise the final phases of the assault cycle described on page 70:

1. Crisis phase — lasting up to 90 minutes after the assault. Adrenalin will still be pumping, the tension gradually abates but is followed by physical and mental exhaustion. This is exemplified by the case of one nurse who was able to finish her night duty after being punched several times while restraining a drunk in the accident department, but the following day found herself lethargic and incapable of coping with even the simplest task.

2. Post-crisis depression — the assault is often interpreted as dehumanising and degrading. In the case of practitioners the depression is often focused upon loss of confidence in their ability to handle any client and loss of a sense of vocation or professional identity. Depression of this sort is often associated with sleeplessness and a pervasive sense of hopelessness.

3. Medium-term effects — overestimating the likelihood of subsequent violence. In the case of practitioners this may be manifested in disproportionate fear of clients, patients or pupils with a violent record, or of situations where violence is likely. They may also be wary of any new situation or new contacts, be no longer willing to confront people because they do not want to face any real risk to themselves, and they may become very apprehensive when people approach from behind. One young teacher, who had been locked in a cupboard for two hours by a bunch of pupils who threatened to burn him alive after he had intervened to stop a fight, explained that he had resigned and gone to another school because he never felt safe in the first school's grounds. But the change of schools had little effect on him: he remained fearful of his charges and finally left the profession.

4. Longer-term effects — being unexpectedly overwhelmed with fear when reliving the traumatic event in the form of intrusive memories or flashbacks, and succumbing to denial of the incident or attempting to erase the feelings associated with it. The effects of an assault may continue to be felt months or even years later, in some cases, long after the physical scars have healed. In this sense, it has much in common with any traumatic event.

It would be a mistake to suppose that these stages of reaction to any serious assault could be easily curtailed. The most sensible self-help strategy is to seek out as much support from others as you can, both in professional circles and from friends or family. Isolating yourself in the hope of dealing with your reactions in secret may simply intensify them. Of course, seeking help has its costs: the loss of self-esteem, the risk of humiliation or of being blamed as a victim. These are discussed further on pages 76–79.

The intensity of the reaction will depend on the nature of the attack and the characteristics of the individual attacked. Assaults differ on a number of dimensions: in the length of time they last (some only moments, others may last days), in the degree of injury inflicted, in the type of injury (physical/emotional/psychological), and so on. There is no consistent pattern of relationships between the characteristics of the assault and the reactions it elicits. The ways in which people's personalities affect their response to assault are more predictable. In their negative reactions to assault, people seem to exaggerate tendencies they already have. So, for instance, the previously anxious person becomes more anxious.

The longevity of the effects of assault will also depend upon the immediate manner in which the incident is handled. The failure by managers to debrief staff who have been involved in an attack may leave the victim with no means of exploring the meaning of the event with someone who understands the nature of their job. This failure to provide an arena in which the incident can be analysed and interpreted is likely to prolong the time it takes the individual to come to terms with it.

FEAR, SURPRISE, ANGER AND GUILT

Rowett (1986) showed that the immediate emotional response to assault is fear, followed by surprise and then anger. But upon the heels of anger comes guilt. This seems to stem from a number of sources.

☐ The assaulted practitioners, though mostly feeling that the incident was unpredictable, believed it to be understandable. While not thinking the incident to be their own fault, neither did they consider it to be solely the client's fault. Instead the majority considered both themselves and the client to be at fault. Guilt can be the product of self-blame. Even if they are unwilling to shoulder the entire responsibility for instigating the attack, they feel partly to blame and acknowledge their guilt. This pattern of results has also been paralleled in studies of schools and hospitals.

☐ The assaulted often think that it is some failing in their professional skills which has made them incapable of defusing the violent situation and preventing the attack. This idea is encouraged by the rhetoric of some employers and some trainers which suggests that once you have been on a training course in handling violence all will be well. It is further supported by the tendency for senior colleagues to keep their own experiences of violence quiet.

☐ Guilt is sometimes generated after the practitioner is attacked more than once. In fact, it seems to be the case that some people are assaulted relatively frequently. In their cases, it may seem a reasonable conclusion that it is something about them which incites attack: perhaps their attitude or ineptitude and guilt might seem appropriate. Of course, such a conclusion may be totally unjustified – it may just be that they work in particularly high-risk areas.

☐ The guilt response is common in many traumatically stressful incidents. For instance, survivors of tragedy where others die often feel guilt despite being innocent of any responsibility for the disaster. The guilt of victims may be a symptom of stress rather than any rational evaluation of responsibility for the event.

Guilt is a debilitating response. It often leads to self-doubt and blame. These in turn destroy confidence and authority. Work becomes a nightmare. Sometimes the loss of confidence spreads out from the victim to colleagues. A community team leader working in social services in an outer London borough described what happened to her team after she was assaulted by a client whom she was trying to move from home into a hostel. She said that the team was shattered. Her main problem as team leader was the loss of authority and the threat posed to the junior members of the team when they recognised that their leader was vulnerable. As she said: 'If I can't protect myself, how can I expect to protect them?' The practitioner sometimes feels guilty not just for having been assaulted but for the incipient threat posed to colleagues.

It may be unrealistic to expect to get over the emotional aftermath of an attack without professional help. Carers have a tendency to avoid using the services of other carers. In this case, seeking counselling help

may be productive, particularly immediately after the incident. Counselling might focus upon the irrationality and damaging impact of
guilt.

VICTIMISATION

The self-blame and guilt which follow an assault may be exacerbated
by the stereotype which is held by the caring professions about those
who fall prey to attack. Rowett (1986) showed that social workers
shared the belief that colleagues who were attacked were provocative,
inexperienced, authoritarian, incompetent, demanding, inflexible and
incapable of detecting the signs of violence in a situation. Similar
stereotypes are produced by nurses and teachers about the members of
their professions who are assaulted. These stereotypes attribute the
blame to the victims. Somehow they are deemed responsible for their
fate. They are pictured as different from their colleagues. The strange
thing is that the *assaulted* also accept the stereotype. They may not
always recognise that it describes them personally, but they are willing
to say that other people who get attacked are like that.

This acceptance of a self-deprecating stereotype is a phenomenon
which occurs in other contexts. Groups which have little power will
accept the stereotype generated about them by more dominant groups
and will believe that they have those characteristics. There is extensive
evidence that before the Black Power movement blacks in the US
accepted the stereotype which deemed them lazy and stupid but at the
same time cunning and childlike. Subordinate groups find it hard to
resist the stereotype which acts to legitimate their powerlessness by
making them seem less worthy of equality. And the stereotype, once
assimilated by a group, can become a self-fulfilling prophecy. Individuals in the group begin to act in ways which accord with the expectations of the stereotype.

Any victim who becomes aware of the stereotype will recognise that
they are considered responsible for their own fate. This awareness of
the beliefs which pervade their own subculture will breed guilt and
self-blame.

But why should such a stereotype exist? It seems in part to be a
manifestation of two biases which are fundamental to the way people
explain what happens in the world. This first bias concerns what are
called 'actor–observer' differences in attribution. If you do something
yourself and are asked to explain it, you are most likely to generate
some explanation in terms of situational constraints or circumstances.

If you watch someone do something and are then asked to explain why he or she did it, you are most likely to produce an explanation in terms of the person's characteristics (their motives, personality, background, etc.). This is the actor–observer difference in its simplest form. When applied to the interpretation of a violent incident, this bias in interpretation will lead to observers' explanations in terms of the characteristics of the assailant and the victim, rather than in terms of the situation or the broader societal framework.

The second bias concerns the 'just world hypothesis'. In explaining events, people seem to suppose that people only get what is coming to them. If something bad happens to you, you must have deserved it. At some level there seems to be a notion that celestial retribution is at work. The 'just world hypothesis' results in victims of crime, for instance, being seen as in some way the originators of their own fate. Most of the research in this area has involved asking people to explain a rape, a mugging or some other violent crime. Most people will attribute responsibility to the victim. The raped woman is assumed to have been flirting or to have a history of promiscuity known to the man. The person who was mugged is supposed to have been wilfully walking in a dangerous area at the wrong time of day or night. The stereotyping of the assaulted carer is merely the routine extension of this process of victimisation.

The stereotype may have arisen because of these general biases in information processing and explanation but it is maintained because it serves a purpose. In attributing blame to the victim the stereotype locates the *control* of violence in the practitioner. Thus violence is not random or fundamentally uncontrollable, it is due to professional inadequacies. This is very reassuring. So long as you are not inadequate, you can expect to remain safe. The stereotype actually protects the majority of practitioners from the truth – which is that anyone can be a victim. People are motivated to accept the stereotype without challenge, for to fail to do so would call into question their own passport to safety.

The existence of the stereotype, and the consequent possibility for victimisation, probably account in large part for the small proportion of violent incidents which is reported. It may also contribute to the difficulties which managers have in providing support for the assaulted after the event. Very few victims report that they receive adequate support from their managers. They describe how their supervisors or managers seem embarrassed in talking about the incident and, how after a very short time, a wall of silence descends. This still seems to be happening, even after the upsurge of publicity about the violence faced by the caring professions and the need for management support.

Victimisation is certainly symptomatic of the more general failure to recognise the structural features which precipitate violence. The individuation of responsibility fudges essential issues. All of the figures indicate that in every caring profession there has been an increase in the number of violent attacks. This cannot be attributed to some sudden decrease in the skills or personal qualities of individual practitioners. The truth of the matter is that the caring professions are being asked to deal with more difficult situations. Teachers are having to handle pupils up to an older age (often against the wishes of the young people, who would rather leave school) and in an economy where they know few will find good jobs as a reward for effort at school. Health service personnel are working in a system which is starved of resources and which cannot hope to provide adequate health care. Social workers, probation officers and health visitors are, as a result of changes in mental health and penal legislation, having to take over the care of people in the community who would previously have been cared for in institutions. These changes in the job descriptions of the caring professions go some way toward explaining the perceived increased incidence of violence. The task facing practitioners is really no longer the same as it used to be.

FACING VICTIMISATION

Victimisation of practitioners should really change to keep abreast of the changing reality, but the problem with stereotypes is of course that they are horrifically difficult to change. Evidence which invalidates them is discounted and exceptions will always be made to the rule if an example really cannot be ignored. This particular stereotype needs to be tackled head on by all members of the caring professions. The first step along the way is for people to realise that they have been accepting the stereotype and to reject it. Then an alternative image must be set up in opposition. This might describe practitioner victims as the frontline troops in society's battle against bad education, poor health and social deprivation, people who regard their own safety as less important than the need to provide a service; and so on. The task is to generate an image which is positive but realistic. Readers might like to list the types of characteristic such an image should contain and consider what evidence could be marshalled to support it if challenged.

In seeking to rectify current victimisation, it would be nonsense to ignore the fact that practitioners sometimes *are* responsible for the ignition of an incident. The object is not to paint practitioners crowned with haloes. It may be true that carers are sometimes involved in the physical abuse of their clients, patients or pupils. There are no large-scale statistics on carer–client violence. It is not the sort of information which would be readily recorded since there are few channels available for clients to voice their complaints. But there is sufficient, well-grounded anecdotal information to make the existence of carer–client violence an undeniable reality (see pages 19–20). There is a great need for independent research to establish the actual magnitude of the problem.

THE ROLE OF THE POPULAR PRESS

Reports of violence are believed to sell newspapers. Reports of violence committed against practitioners are all grist to the mill of the popular press. While reports of practitioner deaths generally present the victim in a sympathetic way, survivors tend to get a rougher ride. The incident is typically sensationalised. The system of values to which most journalists adhere gives priority to novelty and the twist in the tale which will hook the reader. This means that when reporting an attack they will look for whatever is most distinctive, surprising or absurd. Frequently, this means focusing upon the reaction of the practitioner. Anything which is incongruous or suspect will be highlighted.

For instance, in the case of the social worker who was held hostage by a woman with crossbow (see page 68), the press focused upon the fact that he had expressed concern that a message be passed on for his dog to be looked after. This was interpreted as indicating that he did not consider the threat to be serious and was effectively used to minimise the importance of the crime which the woman had committed. The social worker felt that he had been ridiculed by the press. He had been made to seem inadequate for being unable to defuse a minor incident. Yet he had self-consciously used the talk about his dog as a diversionary tactic. Perhaps the most distressing aspect of such press representations is that the 'victim' has virtually no means of redressing the image created.

From a victim's point of view the pattern of reporting in the popular press is likely to reinforce subcultural preconceptions about the character of assaulted practitioners. The press is in effect merely caricaturing the stereotype. By doing so they perpetuate and accentuate it.

There is another issue regarding media coverage of practitioner assaults which needs to be considered. This concerns the likelihood that media coverage of violence to the caring professions will stimulate even more people to be aggressive with practitioners. For some time there has been a debate about the effects of the violence portrayed by the mass media. There seems to be some evidence that watching violence on television is associated with subsequent violence in children. But we do not know whether watching TV violence *causes* children to be violent. There is no similar relationship between *press* coverage of violence and readers' behaviour. There are, of course, exceptions: the so-called copycat crimes. But these are rare. It seems unlikely, therefore, that press reports of assaults against carers will incite additional attacks.

However, there may be a more indirect route from press portrayals to client violence. Members of the caring professions themselves may be influenced by press reports. Their risk estimates may be affected, their general anxiety level may be changed, their perception of particular types of client group may be altered, and so on. These changes may influence their interactions with clients and become self-fulfilling prophecies of violence. The chain reaction is tenuous but it cannot be dismissed. For instance, teachers who see press coverage of surveys into teaching which include graphic examples of violence to give the story 'human interest' are unlikely to ignore the implications for their own classrooms.

After reading this chapter, you might consider doing a rather different sort of self-assessment exercise. Find a current report of an assault against a member of your own profession in the press. Analyse the image of the victim and the image of the assailant. What are represented to be their motives, actions and characteristics? To what extent does the report judge them? How far does the image of the victim comply with the dominant stereotype which has been described above? Then, try to imagine that you are the victim described. How would you react to the coverage? What sort of support would you be looking for from colleagues?

The exercise is meant to help you to read the implicit messages in newspaper reports which you sometimes receive without knowing it. It may also help you to erase your own stereotype of practitioner victims.

Chapter Six

Policy and Management

Management in the caring professions has a role in the response to violence at a variety of levels. Most researchers have stressed the importance of effective management interventions (Strathclyde Regional Council, 1986). The major areas where management can play a part are:

1. In setting up guidelines for practice

2. In supporting staff after an assault

3. In structuring training to deal with violence and its aftereffects

4. In providing technological, organisational and environmental safeguards against assaults.

Each of these areas should be considered in further detail.

GUIDELINES FOR PRACTICE

The actual guidelines for practice which have been developed in the light of the concern about violence differ across professions, of course, because the nature of their work and the context in which it is done vary so greatly. The key thing to emphasise is that management does need to establish guidelines and to circulate them to all staff. These guidelines should at least encompass:

(a) Recommendations about the procedure practitioners should follow when they have estimated that the risk of violence is high (this may include the speed with which supervisors or seniors should be alerted).

(b) Recommendations about the type and extent of back-up necessary for a member of staff making a high-risk contact.

(c) Suggestions about the ways in which cases should be reviewed regularly – including the regular review of long-term clients or patients.

(d) Proposals for the way in which a violent client, pupil or patient should be handled immediately after an incident and in the longer term. Many agencies are now accepting that violence should result in the involvement of the police and prosecution. Where the offence is not serious enough to merit this, guidance is necessary about how to prevent further minor incidents and how the victim is to re-establish effective relations with the assailant. Whatever the sanction used against assailants, potential assailants should be fully aware of their existence.

(e) Recommendations about how any other clients, pupils or patients present at the time of the assault should be counselled or controlled. The effects of a violent act upon others present, who have no immediate part in it, may be considerable. Practitioners need to be briefed on how to manage them. This will differ considerably across professional contexts.

(f) Proposals for the way staff movements can be logged and monitored.

(g) Recommendations for a system which would enable complaints by clients to be investigated and malpractice to be examined. There must be some way of routinely getting the assailant's version of an incident.

(h) Proposals for a system which will facilitate immediate reporting of violent incidents and provide an adequate and easily accessible data base for liaison with other agencies (e.g. the police) and for the staff themselves.

SUPPORT FOR STAFF

After an assault, a debriefing session should be available to all staff. Those assaulted should be encouraged to record all details of the event, this serves both therapeutic and organisational ends. The debriefing would examine in stages what happened and why, how they felt during the incident, what they feel they did wrong and what right, and what they have learned from the experience. Counselling should be made available as a matter of routine. It should be acknowledged that effects may be long term and support should not be curtailed too soon. Managers should be alerted to watch for delayed reactions. Counselling may be best provided outside the person's immediate line management. Victim support schemes may be useful.

Support should include assistance provided to any other members of the team working with the victim. They may need the opportunity to discuss the event together in a relatively structured way and may need to negotiate how they will handle both the assailant and the victim. Facilitating this may seem an obvious management task but it is one which is surprisingly frequently not done.

Support for victims may extend to enabling them to have paid time off work beyond the statutory period. During this time, any problems in getting back to work should be reviewed. Management should provide the victim with the option of refusing further contact with the assailant.

Management should also be responsible for opening access to any compensation scheme available for staff. Victims may be eligible for compensation under the Criminal Injuries Compensation Board as long as the incident is reported to the police. Management must also have a clear policy upon the provision of legal assistance to staff if any prosecution is pursued. Employer insurance should also be established.

STRUCTURED TRAINING

Management has the role of determining what training is needed, and providing it. The route to training need not be conventional. One scheme which has been suggested involves staff exchanges. Effectively, people at similar levels swap jobs for varying periods of time after briefing each other in the complexities of their work. This allows some to get a respite from the continual demands of their own job and gives the opportunity for the exchange of knowledge. Role-play techniques are also highly favoured. The Carolyn Puckett Memorial Fund has employed the theatre group Spanner Workshops to train health visitors. The technique involves establishing a series of scenarios dealing with specific problems: an actor plays the role of the client in a context where the case would be likely to occur, which is outlined to the health visitor. The role-play includes a debriefing with the actor still in role. The scenario is videotaped and analysed later by a group of health visitors and a facilitator. Such techniques could be incorporated into the training of all professional carers.

Training should not only include developing skills in predicting and avoiding or controlling violence, it should also educate the practitioner in the reactions to expect after an assault: the personal emotional response and the reaction of others. There are an increasing number of training packs which can be used for this purpose.

In developing training strategies, it may be useful to highlight the advantages of joint training schemes which take in people from different professional groups. The overwhelming impression gained when the features of attacks and the techniques for avoidance and control are examined is that there are great communalities across professional groups. With the shrinking budgets for training in education, health and social services, it makes economic sense to look for joint training events. It also makes practical sense. Members of these different services frequently have to work together – especially in handling people who are likely to be violent. Subsequent liaison in practice could be facilitated if at least some training were done in common. Such interservice training should sometimes involve the police force since many strategies for containing violence and dealing with its aftermath entail their involvement.

PROVIDING SAFEGUARDS

Safeguards can be provided at the technological, organisational or environmental levels. All must be planned by management. *Technological safeguards* would include personal alarms or mobile telephones. These are costly and there is no clear evidence that they are effective.

Organisational safeguards are rather more complex. For instance, policy on staffing levels might need modification. In the social work context, the Strathclyde report suggested that overreliance on overtime working, part-timers, and poor night cover causes problems; holiday and training commitments need to be taken into account when fixing establishment levels; temporary appointments may need to be encouraged; there may be a need for flexible contracts so that people can move between units; there may be a need to ensure that reception staff are never alone on duty; adequate reporting and recording of incidents may require more clerical staff; the reconsideration of fieldworker staffing levels may be required by the demand for doubling up on visits. There have also been calls from all the caring professions that specialist teams be established to handle dangerous groups of people. This would involve considerable management reorganisation in most contexts.

Environmental safeguards include the redesign of room layouts and furniture provision. Again, these changes often involve massive resource implications. They have to be seen as a part of the development of an overall policy for dealing with violence in a profession.

All these safeguards are directed at protecting the carer. It should also be a priority of management to safeguard those who are cared for. This can only be achieved if management recognises that practitioner violence occurs. Policies need to be evolved for handling practitioner violence when it surfaces. Disciplinary machinery exists in all professional groups for punishing offenders. The problems lie in, firstly, identifying who they are and, secondly, in putting the machinery into action.

The costs to a profession or to an employer involved in disciplining members are very great. There is a strong likelihood that the public will generalise from the incident to other members of the profession or other employees with the consequent loss of credibility and status. The inertia of the system which results may be reinforced where practitioner violence becomes institutionalised. There are scattered reports of violence by staff in residential settings (largely, adolescent treatment centres, old people's homes and hostels for the mentally handicapped). In these settings, an ethos sometimes develops in which violence by staff is acceptable and expected. The violence can be direct brutality or it can be achieved passively through long-term neglect or mistreatment. Either way, it becomes part of the culture of that institution. New staff are socialised into acceptance of it or are pressured into leaving. The problem is that this is a self-perpetuating and self-defending system. Inmates have no way of voicing complaints and staff keep silent in their own interests. The original reasons for the creation of this violent climate may disappear over time but the practices are often maintained for no better reason than habit.

Management has to face the existence of such situations. Policies need to be developed which ensure that residential institutions can be regularly reviewed by independent teams, even in the absence of any complaint. A policy of rotating staff around residential locations may also serve to discourage violent climates.

More generally, individual practitioner violence can probably only be reduced by training programmes which enable staff to understand more of their own motivations towards violence and give them a good grasp of how and when they are most likely to become violent.

THE VALUE OF COLLABORATION

There is some merit in the argument that different management groups in different parts of the country should not be tackling these policy issues independently. There would be considerable advantages in imposing at least some consensual policies. Even across professional groups there is room for managerial dialogue. After all, the professions often have to act in unison.

Conclusion

The book started with a series of questions:

- How frequent are attacks on practitioners?
- What features characterise such attacks?
- How can such attacks be explained?
- What skills are needed in order to deal with attacks and their aftermath?
- What organisational changes would help?

The answers may not have been simple since they have had to encompass a diffuse research literature and explanatory theories from a number of different social sciences. The important thing is that these answers should be of practical value. *Facing Physical Violence* is essentially a summary of existing information: it aims to provide the reader with a basis of knowledge which can subsequently be refined through trial in practice.

In large part, the knowledge gained should be self-knowledge, both for practitioners and managers. Practitioners should have a greater appreciation of the nature and extent of violence and aggression in both their work and non-work lives. They should have a better idea of the forms of violence which they are most likely to exhibit. They should have a clear understanding of any symptoms of stress which they manifest and of how stress levels influence coping abilities. They should be informed about the characteristics of the most likely assailants and be able to use The Dangerousness Checklist in order to assess the risk involved in a contact. They should have mentally rehearsed the strategies they feel they would be personally able to use if faced with an attack situation. They should have explored the value of assertiveness techniques and anxiety management procedures. They should be aware of the likely pattern of reaction in the victim after an assault and how other professionals and society more broadly stereotype the victim. Managers should know the level of risk faced by their staff and have reviewed whether they have actually fulfilled their functions with regard to establishing procedural guidelines, supporting staff, structuring training, and providing safeguards. The caring professions will only be able to face physical violence effectively when both practitioners and managers act in unison with the knowledge they possess.

References

Bandura, A. (1973) *Aggression: A Social Learning Analysis*. Englewood Cliffs, NJ: Prentice Hall.

Berkowitz, L. (1986) *A Survey of Social Psychology*. New York: Holt, Rinehart & Winston.

Brown, R., Bute, S. and Ford, P. (1986) *Social Workers at Risk: The Prevention and Management of Violence*. London: Macmillan.

Crane, D. (1986) *Violence on Social Workers*. Univ. of East Anglia Social Work Monograph 46.

Dollard, J., Doob, L. W., Miller, N. E., Mowrer, O. H. and Sears, R. H. (1939) *Frustration and Aggression*. New Haven, Conn: Yale University Press.

Farrington, D. (1987) Early Precursors of Frequent Offending. In: J. Q. Wilson and G. C. Loury (eds) *From Children to Citizens Vol III*. New York: Springer-Verlag.

Gardner, J. and Gray, M. (1982) Violence Towards Children. In P. Feldman (ed.) *Developments in the Study of Criminal Behaviour Vol. 2*. Chichester: Wiley.

Gorer, G. (1968) Man has no "killier" instinct. In M. F. A. Montague (ed.) *Man and Aggression*. New York: Oxford University Press.

Hampshire Social Services Department (1985) Survey of Violence in Homes for the Elderly, *Research Report No 48*.

Hampshire Social Services Department (1986) *The Prevention and Management of Violence: Staff Guidelines*. Hampshire Social Services Department and Southampton University.

Health Services Advisory Committee (1987) *Violence to Staff in the Health Services*. London: Health and Safety Executive, HMSO.

Home Office (1984) Personal Violence. *Home Office Research Study No. 89*, London: HMSO.

Houghton, S., Wheldall, K. and Merrett, F. (1988) Classroom behaviour problems which secondary school teachers say they find most troublesome. *British Education Research Journal*, 14, 3, 295–310.

Janis, I. L. (1976) Groupthink. In E. Hollander and R. Hunt (eds) *Current Perspectives in Social Psychology*. Oxford: Oxford University Press.

Kahneman, D., Slovic, P. and Tversky, A. (1982) *Judgement Under Uncertainty: Heuristics and Biases*. New York: Cambridge University Press.

Kaplan, S. G. and Wheeler, E. G. (1983) Survival Skills for Working with Potentially Violent Clients. *Social Casework*, 64, 339–346.

Labour Research Department (1987) *Bargaining Report, July*. London: Labour Research Department.

Montagu, A. (1976) *The Nature of Human Aggression*. New York: Oxford University Press.

National Association of School Masters and Union of Women Teachers (1986) *Pupil Violence and Serious Disorder in Schools Survey Report*. London: NASMWT.

Owens, R. G. and Ashcroft, J. B. (1985) *Violence: A Guide for the Caring Professions*. London: Croom Helm.

Rowett, C. (1986) Violence in Social Work. *Institute of Criminology Occasional Paper No 14*, Cambridge University.

Scott, R. L. (1977) Communications as an intentional, social system, *Human Communication Research*, 3, 35–54.

Straus, M. A., Gelles, R. J. and Steinmetz, S. K. (1980) *Behind Closed Doors: Violence in the American Family*. New York: Doubleday.

Surrey County Department (1987) *Safe and Secure in Surrey*. Surrey Social Services Council.

Wheldall, K. and Merrett, F. (1988) The Talkers are the Trouble. *Teachers' Weekly, 21 March*.

Further Reading

Breakwell, G. M. and Rowett, C. (1989) Violence and Social Work. In J. Archer and K. Browne (eds) *Naturalistic Perspectives on Aggression*. London: Routledge.

Finney, G. (1988) One False Move. *Community Outlook*, April.

Freud, S. (1930) *Civilisation and Its Discontents*. London: Hogarth Press.

Lorenz, K. (1966) *On Aggression*. New York: Harcourt, Brace & World.

Marsh, P. and Campbell, A. (eds) (1982) *Aggression and Violence*. Oxford: Blackwell.

Parker, C. and Etherington, S. (1984) *Out of Hours Social Work*. London: British Association of Social Workers.

Poyner, B. and Warne, C. (1985) *Violence to Staff: A Basis for Assessment and Prevention*. London: HMSO.

Siann, G. (1985) *Accounting for Aggression: Perspectives on Aggression and Violence*. Boston: Allen & Unwin.

Tombs, D. (1985) *Guidelines and Recommendations to Employers on Violence against Employees*. London: Association of Directors of Social Services.

Tutt, N. (ed) (1976) *Violence*. London: HMSO.

Wilson, E. O. (1975) *Sociobiology: The New Synthesis*. Boston Mass.: Harvard University Press.

Index

ANCHORING, bias 63
adrenalin 22
aftermath of attack 5, 72-80
  emotions 74-76
  reactions 72-76
  victimisation 76-80
aggression 8, 10
  explanation of 4, 43-50
  outside work 9
  personally preferred forms of 46-48
  tolerable 11-14
  see also violence
anger 18
anxiety management 68
arousal 54
  reduction 18
Ashcroft, J.B. 65
assault cycle 70-71
assertiveness 8, 10
attacks 1-2, 28-42
  aftermath of 5, 72-80
  explanation of 3-4, 43-50
  features of 28, 34-35
  on health workers 2, 28-32
  prediction of 4, 50-55
  on social workers 1-2, 32-40
  on teachers 2, 40-42
  see also violence
availability, bias 61-62
aversive stimulation explanation of
  aggression 45, 48-49
avoidance of violence 5, 57-65
organisational strategies 4, 30-32, 65-
  66, 84-85
prediction of 57-61
risk calculation of 53-55, 61-65

BANDURA, A. 44
Berkowitz, L. 49
Bettridge, Frances 1
bias *see* risk of violence
Birmingham District Health Authority 29
Brown, R. 65

CARING
  professions 7-8, 14-26
  and controlling relationship 14-17
  and emotions 17-18
  and stress 25-26

violence towards clients 19-20, 85
caring relationsip, dangers of 17
causes of attacks *see* explanation
Cembrowicz, Dr 2
child abuse 7, 58
collaboration 86
Confederation of Health Service
  Employees 11
control of violent situation 69-71
controlling relationship, dangers of 14-17
coping with violence 56-71
  avoidance strategies 57-65
  control of 69-71
  environmental strategies 31, 85
  objectives of 56-57
  organisational strategies 4, 30-32. 65-66
  protection and escape 65-69
  self-help strategies 66-67
Crate, D. 65
crime
  and background 58
  and violence 7, 29-30
Criminal Injuries Compensation Board
  83
crowds 51-52
Croydon District Health Authority 29

DANGEROUSNESS CHECKLIST 59
  see also risk calculation
de-individuation 52
displaced violence 16-17
Dollard, J. 48-49
domestic violence

EDUCATION AND VIOLENCE 2, 40-42
elderly people, homes for 39-40
emotions 17-18
  anxiety 68
  and practitioner violence 19-20
  reactions to assault 74-76
  and stress 22
environmental strategies 31, 85
escape 5, 65-69
  see also avoidance; protection
Exeter District Health Authority 29
explanations of aggression and violence
  3-4, 43-50
  aversive stimulation 45, 48-49
  instinct 43-44

social learning 44-45

FARRINGTON, D. 58
Fife District Health Authority 29
frustration-aggression hypothesis 45,
48-49

GARDNER, J. 57
General Adaptation Syndrome 22
Gorer, G. 45
Gray, James 1
Gray, M. 57
groups 51-52
guilt 74-76

HAMPSHIRE SOCIAL SERVICES
DEPARTMENT 39
Health and Safety at Work Act (1974) 4
Health and Safety Commission, report
29-30
Health Service Advisory Committee
30-31
health workers, attacks on 2, 28-32
Home Office, report 29
Hopkins, 73

IMMUNITY, subjective 64-65
instinct explanation of aggression 43-44
institutionalisation 10

JANIS, I.L. 52

KAHNEMAN, D. 61
Kaplan, S.G. 70
killings 1-2

LABOUR RESEARCH DEPARTMENT 37-38
Leeds Social Services Department 38

MANAGEMENT *see* policy and
management
see also organisational strategies
media 79-80
Merrett, F. 41-42
Montagu, A. 7
Morris, Norma 1

NATIONAL ASSOCIATION OF HEAD TEACHERS
41
National Association of Health
Authorities 30
National Association of Schoolmasters
and Union of Women Teachers 2, 40
National Union of Teachers 41
Newcastle District Health Authority 29
newspapers 79-80

ORGANISATIONAL STRATEGIES 4, 30-32,
65-66, 84-85
Owens, R.G. 65

PERSONALLY PREFERRED FORMS OF
VIOLENCE 46-48
police, and violence 29-30
policy and management 81-86
collaboration 86
guidelines for practice 81-82
safeguards 84-86
structured training 83-84
support for staff 82-83
practitioners
violence towards 1-2, 10-11, 14-26, 28-
42, 58-61
violence towards clients 6, 19-20, 85
see also caring professions
prediction of violence 4, 52-55, 57-61
anticipating kind of violence 53-56
risk calculation 53-55, 61-65
towards others 57-58
towards practitioners 58-61
press coverage 79-80
probability calculation *see* risk of
violence
Professional Association of Teachers 42
protection and escape 5, 65-69
anxiety management 68
organisational strategies 65-66
self-help strategies 66-67
Puckett, Carolyn 1
Memorial Fund 83

RAINEY, Jean 2
reactions to assault 16, 72-76
relaxation 27, 68
representativeness, bias 63
restraint, physical 69
risk of violence, calculation of 53-55, 61-
65
Rowett, C. 32-34, 37, 74, 76
Royal College of Nursing 30

SAFEGUARDS 84-86
schools, violence in 2, 40-42
Schwarz, Isabel 1
Scott, R.L. 7
self-assessment exercises 6
aggression and violence outside work 9
dangerousness checklist 59
features of attacks 34-35
personally preferred forms of
aggression or violence 46-48
stress checklist 22-23
tolerable aggression and violence 12-13

victim stereotyping 80
self-help strategies 66-67
situations, interpreting 50-51
social learning explanation of
   aggression 44-45
social workers, attacks on 1-2, 32-40
   assailants 33, 35-36
   context 35-36
   victims, 34, 36, 76-77
Spanner Workshops 83
stereotype of victims 76-80
Strathclyde Regional Council 38, 65,
   81, 84
Straus, M.A. 7
stress 20-27
   and caring professions 25-26
   causes of 21-22
   checklist 22-23
   coping with 25-27
   effects of 22-25
subjective immunity 64-65
support for staff 31, 82-83
Surrey Social Services Department 39

TEACHERS, attacks on 2, 40-42
'time-outs' 70
tolerable aggression 11-14
training, structured 83-84

VICTIMISATION 36, 76-80
violence 8
   aftermath of 5, 72-80
   see also attacks
   avoidance of 57-65
   and caring 7-8, 14-26
   control of 69-71
   coping with 56-71
   displaced 16-17
   domestic 7
   in education 2, 40-42
   explanation of 3-4, 43-50
   and groups 51-52
   in the health services 1-2, 28-32
   kinds of 52-55
   as occupational hazard 10-11, 14
   outside work 9
   personally preferred forms of 46-48
   policy and management 81-86
   by practitioners 6, 19-20
   prediction of 4, 50-55, 57-65
   protection and escape 65-69
   in the social services 1-2, 32-40
   and stress 20-24
   tolerable 11-14

WHEELER E.G. 70
Wheldall, K. 41-42
wife battering 7